The Firehouse Grilling Cookbook

The Firehouse Grilling Cookbook

150 GREAT GRILLING RECIPES PLUS SAFETY TIPS

Joseph T. Bonanno Jr.

BROADWAY BOOKS / NEW YORK

BROADWAY

Broadway Books titles may be purchased for business or promotional use or for special sales. For information, please write to: Special Markets Department, Bantam Doubleday Dell Publishing Group, Inc., 1540 Broadway, New York, NY 10036.

BROADWAY BOOKS and its logo, a letter B bisected on the diagonal, are trademarks of Broadway Books, a division of Bantam Doubleday Dell Publishing Group, Inc.

Library of Congress Cataloging-in-Publication Data
Bonanno, Joseph T.
The firehouse grilling cookbook : 150 great grilling recipes plus safety tips / Joseph T. Bonanno, Jr. — 1st ed.
p.   cm.
Includes index.
ISBN 0-7679-0098-7
1. Barbecue cookery.   I. Title.
TX840.B3B58   1998   97-47507
641.5′784-dc21   CIP

FIRST EDITION

Designed by Richard Oriolo

98 99 00 01 02 10 9 8 7 6 5 4 3 2 1

This book is dedicated to the twelve New York firefighters who died in the line of duty since the publication of The Healthy Firehouse Cookbook in 1995, as well as the many other firefighters who have died from job-related illnesses. It is also dedicated to my good friend and firefighter, Gary Dempsey of Engine 273, and James Myerjack of the fitness unit, who succumbed to cancer in 1997. It is also dedicated to the memory of my dear Uncle Ted, who taught me so much, both in the kitchen and out. May God rest their souls.

Contents

Acknowledgments

Since my first cookbook, there are many people in the publishing and public relations worlds who have made a difference in my life, and their kind words keep me going.

First and foremost, I would like to thank Rick Rodgers for helping with this book from the ground up. I call him "The Food King." He had immeasurable input in my first book, making it a success, and he has done it again with this one. Rick's assistants, Diane Kniss and Steven Evasew, literally kept the home fires burning with this book.

I never thought that as a firefighter, I would need an agent, but now I have one of the best, Susan Ginsburg. Thanks to Gary Goldberg, whose New School course, "How to Write a Cookbook," helped me turn an idea into two actual books. Harriet Bell, my editor, has worked with me on both, and I am grateful for her support. I also want to thank Stephanie Richardson of the Barbecue Industry Association for her researching assistance. Betty Hughes from Weber-Stephens generously donated grills for the recipe testing. Special thanks to Antoinette and Wilma, Cynthia, Valerie, and Donna and the Sunnyside girls, Diane, Beth, and Kellie. They know why.

My sincerest thanks to all the members of my new firehouse, Engine 299 and Ladder 152, in Fresh Meadows, Queens, New York City, and all the surrounding companies in Battalion 52. They're not only a great bunch of firefighters, but accomplished food critics as well.

Finally, very special thanks to all the firefighters who took the time to send me recipes—and keep them coming!

Introduction

Since *The Healthy Firehouse Cookbook* came out three years ago, I have been overwhelmed by the positive response from firefighters and the general public who enjoyed the healthy recipes I collected from America's firehouses. There are many things that I like about my job as a New York City firefighter, but many of my nicest memories come from sitting around the dinner table with my fellow firefighters enjoying great food with good company. I think one of the reasons firefighters have such a love for good food is they know that life's pleasures can be cut short in an instant. There is a sign in a Bronx firehouse that says, "This Could Be the Night!"

As I traveled around the country promoting my cookbook, I got to dine at many firehouses. The locations and faces changed, but the firefighters all had the same sense of humor and love for their jobs. They were also great cooks. I noticed that many of the firehouse meals were being cooked with an eye to health. The firefighters had heard the message from the media about trimming dietary fat, but when they heard it from one of their own, they took it to heart.

I also noticed that grilling was the most popular way for the firefighters to cook. Many firehouses give annual barbecues to raise money for their departments. Chicken barbecues are the most popular. (In fact, there's a classic chicken marinade recipe on page 152 that has been passed from station to station.) In my first book, many of the recipes sent to me by firefighters were for the grill. When I started to think about what kind of book the sequel should be, the answer was clear—grilling.

Grilling is a low-fat cooking method by nature, as it gives lots of flavor to food without adding fat. Some of the flavor comes from the smoke, and some comes from the dark brown, caramelized crust the hot fire imparts to the food's surface. Marinades, salsas, barbecue sauces, and spice rubs play important roles in grilling, and they can be low in fat, too (if you cut way back on the oil in the marinades, which is what I have done). Grilling has always been popular during the warm-weather months, but now that more and more people own gas grills, cooks are grilling year-round, and there's no end in sight to the trend.

I think healthy cooking has become second nature to American cooks, whether they work in a fire department or at a department store. They understand the concept of balancing indulgent foods with healthy ones, reducing fat intake, increasing exercise, and adding more fish, grains, and vegetables to their diets. They are cooking from low-fat recipes they find in food magazines and cookbooks. So, for this book, I decided to ask for my fellow firefighters' favorite recipes for grilled foods (and side dishes and picnic desserts), without any regard for their final fat gram count. Just as I expected, a lot of the submitted recipes were low in fat without consciously attempting to be so.

Also, as I suspected, most of the side dishes and desserts were not low in fat. But, not *every* bite you take has to derive less than 30 percent of its calories from fat. Many nutritionists recommend that we stick to dietary guidelines 70 percent of the time, and allow ourselves treats the rest of the time. If you want a low-fat salad or dessert, look in one of those other good cookbooks (including *The Healthy Firehouse Cook Book)*—although you will find a few here.

I can't believe that I am nearing twenty years in the New York Fire Department. Love it or hate it, New York is an exciting place to be, and an even more exciting place to be a firefighter. I am convinced that many of the good things that have happened to me in the last few years occurred because I was in the right place at the right time—and that right place was New York City. It enabled me to become a published author, sharing good cooking and fire safety with lots of new people. And I got to know my fellow firefighters better in the process, usually around a delicious meal—I wouldn't have it any other way.

Taming the Flame: Grilling Basics

Grilling has fast become Americans' favorite way to cook. For many firefighters, it seems to be the *only* way to cook. I swear, if they could figure out how to cook their pasta sauce on a barbecue, they would! It's odd—we spend all day fighting the "Red Devil" (our nickname for fire), yet when we get home, we light up the grill. In my case, I guess I want to be reminded that fire can be a humankind's friend, too. And, man, does that grilled food taste good!

Until recently, unless you lived in a sunny climate, you had to wait for warm weather to grill your favorite foods. Now, thanks to gas grills, people are grilling 365 days a year. In fact, sales of gas grills are neck-and-neck with sales of charcoal grills. Because there are differences between gas and charcoal grills, I have included directions for both types in these recipes. After all, it's feasible that you cook on only one kind of grill and don't know how to automatically adjust the recipe to the other kind. Most cookbooks give instructions for only one grill, but I bet that more will give both sets of instructions as the years go by and gas grills become even more common.

If you are thinking of purchasing a grill, I can't advise you that gas is better than charcoal or vice versa. There are more criteria, such as where you live, how many people you normally cook for, and your level of cooking expertise. I will say that while gas grilling is more convenient (no igniting coals or concerns about dumping the used ones, and controlling the temperature with the turn of a dial), charcoal-grilled food does have more flavor—although most people won't find the difference dramatic. Grill masters love to argue with me about this. "I tell you, Joe, you *can't* taste the difference!" My answer is they probably haven't had the opportunity to taste the same recipe cooked side-by-side in gas and charcoal as I have (or at least with the recipes in this book). The cause for the difference is simple: Gas grills do not cook as hot as charcoal, so they don't brown the exterior of the food as well. It is this browned, caramelized surface that gives grilled food its distinctive flavor, as well as the smokiness imparted by the charcoal. (Yes, you can add wood chips to a gas grill to add smoke, but the food still won't get as browned.) So, if you are a traditionalist, and want the best-tasting grilled food you ever put a fork to, regardless of the extra time needed to deal with the coals and learning how to tame the flame, get a charcoal grill. If your lifestyle calls for doing things the easy way, and you are accustomed to the milder flavor of gas-grilled foods (and they are excellent on their own terms), get a gas grill. Perhaps most important, I just don't want people to forget what real charcoal-grilled food tastes like.

There is such an animal as an electric grill. If a gas grill burns a bit lower than a charcoal grill, electric grills burn even lower than that. For people who just can't have either gas or charcoal (perhaps because of some regulations where they live), electric grills are a distant third option, but they are not addressed in this book at all.

Now let's talk about each grill, and how to use them to make great grilled meals.

Charcoal Grills

From large kettle grills that can barbecue a flock of chicken for a crowd to small hibachi grills for grilling up just a couple of burgers, charcoal grills were responsible for igniting America's love affair with outdoor cooking.

Types of Charcoal Grills

Most charcoal grills are *covered kettle grills*. They are round with tight-fitting lids and adjustable air vents in the lid and on the bottom of the grill. There are two grates—the small one holds the charcoal, and the large one holds the food. The kettle shape ensures good heat distribution and air flow, which is important because oxygen helps keep a fire alive (that's what those air vents are for). While no-frills models work fine, good manufacturers, like Weber-Stephen, offer well-designed features to make grilling more efficient. These include cup-shaped ash catchers, hinged flaps for the cooking grate to make it easier to add coals to the fire as it burns down, and lid thermometers to gauge the interior temperature of the grill. These features may seem extraneous, but once you've gotten used to them, you'll realize how great they are, so try to budget them in.

The grill lid should be closed to trap the heat, effectively turning your grill into an outdoor oven that cooks the food in the shortest time possible. Usually the cooking grate is stationary, and the amount of heat is regulated by the intensity of the charcoal fire. Kettle grills easily can be converted to allow for smoking food. All the charcoal-grilled recipes in this book were tested on a kettle grill.

Braziers are square or rectangular grills. Sometimes they have lids, but often not. They typically have adjustable cooking grates that can be lowered or raised over the coals to adjust the amount of heat applied to the food. In general, kettle grills heat better and are sturdier.

Hibachis and *tabletop grills* are great for small meals. Their size won't allow for smoking food. Hibachis may not have covers, but they are a good choice for grilling just a side dish of zucchini or a couple of chicken breasts. (You can always cover the food with a tent of heavy-duty aluminum foil to contain the heat.) Tabletop grills usually have lids and can be transported easily. If you are a serious smoked-food fan, you will want to have a hibachi or small tabletop grill just for igniting the coals that must be added to a fire to maintain the optimum temperature as it burns down. (More about this under Direct, Indirect, and Banked-Coal Grill-Cooking, below.)

Some firefighters who are going for the grilling gold have huge *drum grills*. These used to be homemade affairs, often made from old oil drums and metal fencing cut to size for a cooking grate. Now they can be purchased at many outdoor furniture shops. They call for special cooking skills, and we won't discuss them in this book. But, if you are really into grilling, and usually cook for a lot of people, you might want to have one.

Types of Fuel

Not so long ago, when it came to charcoal, the cook had no choice—charcoal briquettes were the only choice. Now there are flavored briquettes, real charcoal, and self-lighting briquettes. There is even one charcoal grill that has a small propane tank attached to use for lighting the coals.

Charcoal briquettes are the most popular and common grill fuel, and for good reason. The briquettes are evenly shaped and yield predictable amounts of heat. They are made from pulverized charcoal mixed with binders and pressed into the familiar pillow shape. Buy the best brand you can, as some inexpensive brands use a higher proportion of binding agents, which make the briquettes burn "dirty," casting a thin layer of black ash over the food.

Flavored briquettes have pulverized wood, such as mesquite, added to the charcoal mixture, so the wood flavor is automatically added to the food as the fire burns. They are great when you want smoked flavor without the bother of adding wood chips.

Self-lighting briquettes have been coated with a lighting fluid to ensure easy ignition. Some cooks like them, but with all the safe, easy ways to light fires, I stay away from any lighting fluids, which are the cause of many grilling accidents. If you do use these (and I do not recommend them), light them in a single layer, not in a mound, and never use any secondary ignition method, such as an electric starter or a chimney. Most important, never add them to an existing fire, or the lighting fluid may give an off-flavor to the food.

Hardwood charcoal is the real McCoy. Irregularly shaped pieces of true hardwood charcoal (not pulverized charcoal and without binders) can be purchased in large bags at well-supplied houseware or hardware shops. The type of wood processed into charcoal changes with the location of the plant. Northwestern charcoal tends to be oak, and western (especially Texan) is often mesquite. Hardwood charcoal adds a wonderful flavor to cooked foods, but it has its quirks. It burns much hotter than briquettes and burns out more quickly. It is also hard to control the heat of a hardwood charcoal fire, as large pieces will give off more heat than small ones. It is best for fast-cooking foods like beef steaks, burgers, or fish steaks. If you want to use it for longer-cooked foods, mix it with briquettes to extend the life of your fire and even out its heat.

Surefire Lighting Techniques

For inexperienced cooks, lighting a charcoal fire can seem daunting. There are many surefire ways—and none of them include using dangerous lighting fluid. Too many grill cooks, even good ones, turn into wild-eyed pyromaniacs when it comes time to light the fire, and that's how accidents happen. Also, lighting fluids can give a lighting-fluid-taste to foods. (It is said that the flavor burns off, but if that's so, why do we all know what lighting-fluid-flavored chicken tastes like?) There's no need to use lighting fluid, so don't.

How much charcoal should you use? For a typical grilling job, use about five pounds for a $22^1/_2$-inch round kettle grill. No, you don't have to weigh the coals—just estimate a quarter of a twenty-pound bag (or, of course, half of a ten-pounder). Less charcoal is required for indirect cooking.

No matter what cooking method you use, allow twenty to thirty minutes for the fire to ignite and burn to the point where the charcoal is covered with a layer of white ash. If you add the food to the grill before the coals are covered with ash, the black areas of the briquettes could give off ashes and noxious fumes as they ignite and contaminate your food. And don't try to light a fire with the grill lid closed—it cuts off the oxygen, and fires need oxygen to breathe, just like humans.

Using a Chimney Starter. My favorite way to light a fire is with a chimney starter, now available at just about every hardware store and kitchen shop in the nation. These all-metal containers have two compartments, one for the charcoal, and one for crumpled newspaper. The newspaper is lighted, which in turn lights the coals. In about twenty minutes . . . bingo! Beautifully ignited coals. All chimney starters are not created equal. Buy the largest, sturdiest one you can (it should hold a full five pounds of briquettes) and be sure it is made from rustproof metal.

Using Newspaper Knots. This simple, efficient method uses newspaper, tied into knots, as kindling. You'll wonder why more people don't use it. Take a double thickness of newspaper (use a double-page section that opens to 27 inches wide). Starting at a long end, roll up tightly into a cylinder. Tie the paper cylinder into an overhand knot and set aside. Make three or four newspaper knots in this fashion. Place the newspaper knots on the very bottom of the kettle. Set the metal charcoal grate in place over the knots. Mound the charcoal on the center of the grate. Using long fireplace matches, light the newspaper. The thick newspaper knots will take a few minutes to burn down and act as nonchemical kindling.

Using Solid Starters. Solid, odorless cubes of fuel are another way to go, but there's no reason to become dependent on them when the above methods are so easy. Place a fuel cube on the charcoal grate, and build a pyramid of coals over the cube, leaving a corner of the cube exposed. Light the cube, and it will do the rest.

Using Electric Starters. Why anyone would want to depend on having an electric source outside to light a grill is beyond me. With electric starters, there are also too many fire safety concerns.

How Hot Is Hot?

Cooking with charcoal is all about regulating the heat. Just treat your outdoor grill somewhat like an indoor stove. For example, some foods you simmer over low heat, and others are better cooked over high heat. It's the same thing in a grill. Most people like their steaks with a rich brown crust that can be formed only by the high heat radiated from freshly lit coals (but be sure they are covered with white ash before adding the food). More delicate foods are best cooked over coals that have burned down to medium-high. How the coals are arranged will make a difference in heat distribution, too. If the coals are heaped in a mound, they will give off more heat than if they are spread out.

To gauge the temperature of the fire, hold your hand just above the cooking grate. If the fire is *hot*, you should be able to hold your hand over the coals for one to two seconds. If you can hold your hand over the coals for three to four seconds, the fire is *medium-hot*. If you can hold your hand over the fire for longer than five seconds, not only is the fire *medium*, but it also may be too cool for grilling the food, and you may want to add some fresh coals and let them ignite before proceeding. To increase the heat of a fire that has burned down without adding more coals, protect your hands with long oven mitts and use a long-handled garden trowel or another tool to push the coals together.

Top-of-the-line grill models have a thermometer in their lids to give a temperature reading. These are especially helpful when long-cooking foods. If you don't have this feature on your grill, place an inexpensive oven thermometer next to the food to get a reading. I suggest an inexpensive thermometer as it can discolor from the smoke, although that often can be scrubbed off with a steel-wool cleaning pad.

Adjusting the air vents is one of the most effective ways to regulate the heat. Fires need oxygen to keep them alive. Most models have vents on the top and the bottom to give you lots of control over the oxygen flow. If you open the vents wide, the amount of oxygen is increased, and the fire will burn its quickest and hottest. If you close the vents to decrease the oxygen, the fire will burn more slowly and at a lower temperature. In general, keep the vents open most of the time, and close them after grilling when you want to stifle the fire.

If the recipe calls for covering the grill with the lid (and most of them do), don't open the lid more than necessary or the heat will escape. Like the argument over the superiority of gas versus charcoal, grill cooks love to fight it out over covered versus uncovered grilling. Some cooks say that food grilled with the lid closed tastes steamed, which is hogwash, in my opinion. If your grill is clean, especially the inside of the lid, you should have no problems with any off-flavors.

For information on dealing with flare-ups, see page 17.

Keeping It Clean

At least once a year, and even more if you grill frequently, clean the grill. You can spray the inside of the kettle and the lid with oven cleaner. Or scrub it clean with a steel-wool cleaning pad. Another way is to hose down the grill with water, and scrub it with generous sprinkles of baking soda and an old sponge (the sponge will be useless after rubbing off the accumulated grease). Wash the outside with soap and water, too. Invest in a good cover to protect the grill during inclement weather and for storing during cold months.

Gas Grills

Gas grills use liquid propane for their fuel source. Some people have their grills hooked up to permanent gas lines, but most use propane tanks attached to the grill. Gas grills are popular for their ease of operation and convenience.

Gas Grill Options. There are a number of options to consider when purchasing a gas grill. Price will always be a factor, but, as with so many other things, where gas grills are concerned, you get what you pay for.

Cooking Surface Size. Get the largest cooking surface you can afford, at least three hundred fifty to four hundred square inches. Even if you usually cook small amounts of food, a small cooking surface will really trip you up if you want to cook more than one thing at a time.

Amount of BTUs. BTUs (British thermal units) are the units that measure how hot your grill gets. Most grills generate 20,000 to 50,000 BTUs. If your grill will be located where it is windy and cool (perhaps on a terrace), you will want a grill to generate a greater amount of BTUs to compensate for the breeze cooling the grill. (Also, those breezes can be annoyingly pesky and blow out the gas flame of less powerful models.) On the other hand, some gas grills burn so high that you can't adjust the heat to lower temperatures, and you can use it only for high-temperature grilling of steaks and chops. The best advice is to buy your gas grill from a reliable dealer who can inform you about the different models and their heating efficiency.

Heating Elements. Most gas grills have two burners that are installed side-by-side. If you want high heat, you turn on both burners. If you are cooking by the indirect method (discussed below), you turn one side on and the other side off, cooking the food on the "off" side of the grill, and allowing the heat radiated by the other side to do the cooking. Usually these grills use lava rocks or ceramic briquettes to radiate heat. As these will get soaked with cooking fat, replace them annually to discourage any grease fires or off-flavors.

Weber-Stephen gas grills have three sets of metal plate burners that run horizontally, front-middle-back. They do not have lava rocks or ceramic briquettes, and as the food's juices drip onto the hot metal plates, smoke that flavors the food is created. When you want to cook by the indirect method, the middle burner can be turned off, and the front and back burners kept on. While this makes for good heat distribution, Weber gas grill owners will probably find that indirectly cooked food will be done a little sooner on these grills than other grills, and may have to adjust standard cooking times.

How Hot Is Hot?

In a gas grill, temperatures can be adjusted with the twist of a thermostat. However, there are still variables to consider.

First of all, always preheat your grill with the burners on high for at least 15 minutes before adding the food. (When you turn on the grill, leave the lid open; in case the flame doesn't ignite, you won't have gas accumulating under the lid.) Not only does preheating ensure that your grill gets up to the proper cooking temperature, it also heats the cooking grate so it will sear the food with those appetizing crisscrosses that are the mark of a real grill master. Always cook with the lid closed to keep the heat contained.

The weather will definitely affect the grilling temperature. Cool breezes will chill the grill's metal casing and cause the interior heat to drop. You can compensate by turning up the grill, but sometimes the grill never gets hot enough, even on the highest setting.

If you have a flare-up, turn the grill off. Remove the food from the grill. Wait 5 minutes before relighting the grill, and then put the food back on the cooking grate.

Direct, Indirect, and Banked-Coal Grill-Cooking

Too many backyard cooks confuse grilling with pyromania. They toss a piece of meat onto the grill without any regard for the fat dripping onto the coals and causing flare-ups. In fact, this kind of cook considers the flare-up the point of grilling, because it turns a simple cooking technique into a cosmic battle of human against fire. Not only is this unsafe thinking, but it doesn't make for delicious food, either.

There's more than one way to grill food. In fact, there are three separate grilling methods to be applied according to the food you wish to cook.

When you cook food directly over hot coals, you are using the *direct method*. Direct cooking works best for foods that take less than 25 minutes to cook through, such as beef steaks, chops, burgers, sausages, and fish steaks. This is actually "grilling."

Some foods are cooked by the *indirect method*. I use this technique with a lot of recipes, because it is actually more versatile than direct grilling. With indirect cooking, only one side of the grill is heated, and the other side left empty and unlit. The food is placed on the empty side of the grill and the lid is closed. (Some cooks prefer to spread out the fire to either side of the grill and place the food in the center, between the two small fires, but it's not really necessary to add that extra step.) The fire heats the inside of the grill, and the food cooks from the radiated heat. Sometimes, as with my charcoal method for cooking poultry, the fire is left in the center of the grill in a mound, and the poultry is arranged around, but not over, the coals. Often, I will place a disposable aluminum foil pan on the empty side of the grill and fill it halfway with water or another liquid that will add flavor as it steams. Not only does the steam help to keep the food moist, but the fat drips into the water and helps during cleanup as well. Indirect grill-cooking is very useful, as it prevents the food from burning before it is cooked through. In addition to using it in many poultry recipes, I use it for large pieces of meat.

A charcoal fire will eventually burn down and become too cool to cook over. If you are cooking for longer than 45 minutes, you will have to add more coals to the fire. The coals should be ignited and covered with white ash, as black, unlit briquettes will take too long to ignite and will give off ashes as they do so. Light the auxiliary coals in a hibachi or small stovetop grill. Carefully transfer them to the large grill with spring-action kitchen tongs or a small metal trowel. Some grills have hinged flaps or openings at the handles that should be positioned over the fire to to make the transferring easier.

To use the indirect method on most gas grills, you just turn one burner on, and leave the other burner off. If you have a Weber grill, you leave the middle burner off, and leave the top and bottom burners on. The food is placed over the area of the grill that is not lit. It is usually a good idea to place a foil pan underneath the food, directly on the heat source, to catch any drips.

The *banked coal method* combines indirect and direct grilling. After the fire has ignited, the mound is banked, with one side about three or four coals high, slanting to a single layer of coals. The food is seared over the hot, high-banked coals, then moved over the cooler, shallow layer of coals to continue cooking without the high risk of scorching. With gas grills, there is a variation where the food is seared over high heat, then the heat is reduced to medium or low to cook the food through. Use this method for cuts like leg of lamb, where food should be crusty on the outside, yet would cause flare-ups if allowed to cook directly over the flames.

There is another technique that deserves mention. Even though many of us use the words "barbecue" and "grilling" interchangeably, they are, in fact, very different procedures. Grilling is direct cooking. *Barbecuing* is a form of indirect cooking. It uses very low heat and lots of aromatic smoke to flavor the meat. The lack of heat involved makes for long, slow cooking. Different regions have different barbecuing traditions, based on what meats and woods are available. For example, in the Carolinas, you'll find hickory-smoked pork shoulder barbecue with a vinegar baste. In Texas, the favorite is beef brisket smoked with mesquite, served with a tangy tomato sauce (or plain, since it's so good). In the Deep South, ribs are the order of the day, preferably smoked with peach wood, and don't be surprised if there's some Coca-Cola in the sauce—although I prefer a simple sweet tomato sauce. We even have our own kind of barbecue in the Northeast, but we call it a clambake. It may use clams instead of meat, but it's still a kind of barbecue.

Adding Flavor: Smoke, Marinades, and Spice Rubs

Today's American tastebuds can handle a lot of flavor. Take salsa. Just ten years ago, you only found it at Mexican restaurants. Now it is more popular than tomato ketchup.

As people started grilling more at home, they noticed that their home-grilled meals didn't have the smoky flavor that they enjoyed at restaurants. So, wood chips became a common addition to backyard grilling.

Aromatic hardwoods, such as hickory, mesquite, and oak, are great ways to add flavor to grilled foods. They can be found at many hardware stores and kitchenware shops. Regional favorites, like peach, apple, cherry, maple, pecan, and sassafras, aren't easily available outside their localities, so I'll leave them out of the discussion. If you are thinking of using wood from your property, stay away from resinous woods such as pine, as it produces smoke that is too strongly flavored, and be sure the cut wood is aged and dried.

There are two types of wood available: small *wood chips* and large *wood chunks*. The chips are best for foods that will cook in a relatively short period of time—let's say 30 to 45 minutes. Chunks work well for long-cooked foods, because they don't burn as quickly as chips and you won't have to open the lid to add more as often.

Wood chips or chunks are always soaked in water for at least 30 minutes and then drained well before they are added to the grill. (You can soak the wood for a few hours, if you wish.) Soaked wood will smolder and smoke before burning. Drain any leftover wood and spread it out to dry for another use. If the wood is allowed to stay moist, it can become moldy and will be unusable.

If you have a charcoal grill, just toss a big handful of the drained chips or a few chunks onto the coals. Cover the grill and wait until the chips smolder and build up a good head of smoke (you'll see it seeping out of the air vents) before adding the food to the cooking grate. Add more wood when you don't see any more smoke, which usually happens after 30 to 35 minutes.

Gas grills are a bit troublesome, because you don't want the ashes from the wood chips to clog the burner vents. But there are many easy solutions. The simplest remedy is to purchase a metal chip box that fits your grill model. (Call the grill manufacturer to see if they have one available by mail order.) The box is permanently installed into your gas grill, and the wood smolders in the box without touching the heat source. Or, wrap the wood in a double thickness of aluminum foil, pierce a few holes in the foil, and place the foil packet directly on the heat source—the foil will protect the heat source from the ashes. You can also place a small aluminum foil tray on the heat source, and place the wood in the tray (many bags of wood chips come with a foil tray included). In any case, cover the grill and let the wood build up a head of smoke. Be patient, as it will take somewhat longer for the wood to start smokin' in a gas grill than in a charcoal grill.

Experience has shown that certain woods work best with certain foods. While you can certainly experiment, there is a rule of thumb. Strong-flavored woods like mesquite and hickory will enhance full-flavored foods like beef, salmon, and pork. Sweet, mild fruit woods go well with poultry and many pork products, too. Here are some suggestions for the most commonly available woods:

- Alder: A favorite in the Northwest, it is perfect with salmon and shellfish.

- Hickory: Usually used for Carolina-style pork, it's a good all-purpose wood for poultry, beef, and seafood, too.

- Mesquite: Mesquite and beef are a great combination, but try it with rich-flavored fish steaks such as tuna, salmon, and swordfish, as well as pork and poultry.

- Oak: Use this to add a European flavor to your food. It works well with just about every kind of food, but especially pork and sausage.

There are lots of other things you can toss onto your grill to add flavor. Some suggestions include heads of garlic (cut in half and don't soak first), herbs (basil stems stripped of leaves, rosemary sprigs, soaked and drained bay leaves or fennel seeds), citrus peels, and corn cobs (let them dry out for a few days before using with pork chops). Don't be surprised if these additions are more style than substance. They smell wonderful, but unless you let their smoke come in contact with the food for longer than 30 minutes, they may not add a lot of flavor.

Marinades are another way to add an extra flavor dimension to grilled foods. There are two common mistakes that cooks make with marinades: using too much oil in the marinade and overmarinating the food.

Most old marinade recipes start out with one cup of oil. That's way too much! There should be only enough oil in the recipe to lubricate the meat and help keep it from sticking to the cooking grate. Besides, unless you are using a flavorful oil like extra-virgin olive oil, most oils are tasteless, so all you are adding to the recipe are unwanted fat grams and fuel for flare-ups. My marinade recipes use a minimum of oil. With your old recipes, try cutting back on the oil by one-third to one-half—you won't miss it at all.

Because my marinades are less oily, they are stronger and more acidic. Take care not to overmarinate the food, or the acids could break it down and affect the texture. Although some recipes allow for longer marinating periods, 8 hours is enough for firm-textured meats like beef and pork, 6 to 8 hours is enough for poultry, and 1 hour is plenty for seafood.

While spice rubs have been around for a long time, they have been recently discovered by grill cooks. You can buy a number of spice rubs at the market, but I prefer to make my own because I can delete salt, MSG, and preservatives from the blend. If you use a spice rub, be sure to brush the meat with oil first, to moisten the spices and keep them from scorching.

A Word About Timing

It's exasperating when you ask a buddy how long it takes to cook something, and he says, "Until it's done." But, with grilling, I sometimes wonder if that isn't the most accurate description.

There are many variables that affect the final cooking time of grilled food. It's not really a problem, as long as you're aware that they exist and you take them into account. Weather is the first factor. If it is cold or breezy, the metal casing will get cold, and the interior temperature of the grill will drop. With gas grills, the exact thermostat settings of High, Medium, and Low change from model to model, and some of them have "hot spots," just like an oven. If you open the lid too often, and let the heat escape, that will change the timing, too. Also, be sure to use about 5 pounds of briquettes for a typical grilling job so you start with the same amount of fuel that I used during testing. But don't worry—I always include a visual test or an instant-read temperature reading to help you tell when the food is done, even if the timing gets thrown off.

Keeping Cool: Grilling Safety Tips

More people are grilling than ever before. And the more people grill, the higher their confidence levels climb, sometimes to the point that they become careless. Lighting up a barbecue is not unlike driving a car—it's safe, as long as you pay attention to what you are doing and adhere to a few rules.

As a firefighter, fire safety is one of my biggest concerns. Here are some important tips, rules, and guidelines to be sure you grill the best way—safely!

General Grilling Safety Tips

- Before you use your grill, read the owners' manual to be aware of any specific safety concerns about your model. If you have any questions about your grill, feel free to contact the grill manufacturer.

- *Never* use a grill in an enclosed area, such as a trailer, tent, house, or garage. Set up the grill in a well-ventilated area. Grills are designed for outdoor use *only.* Carbon monoxide is invisible, and it can easily build up in an enclosed area and kill you. Yes, kill you.

■ Set up the grill in an open area, away from buildings, dry leaves, brush, or overhanging tree branches. Watch out for wind-blown fire sparks.

■ Do not set up the grill in a high-traffic area. The body of the grill becomes very hot without looking hot, and it is easy for someone casually walking through (or if kids are around, they will probably be running through) to accidentally touch the hot surface and get burned.

■ If you are using electrically operated accessories, such as rotisseries, be sure they conform with local codes and are grounded properly. Keep the cords away from the walkway. If possible, tape the cords down with duct tape to prevent tripping.

■ Use long-handled barbecue tools to avoid burns and splatter. Oven or barbecue mitts, preferably long and flame retardant, are very helpful, too.

■ Don't wear long, floppy shirtsleeves that could accidentally catch fire. On the other hand, even if it's hot, wear enough clothing to protect your body from accidental burns—cooking in your bathing suit is not a good idea.

■ Never attempt to move a hot grill.

■ Know where the nearest fire extinguisher is located. Have a garden hose hooked up and handy, just in case.

Charcoal Grilling Safety Tips

■ Build your fire without charcoal igniting fluid, according to the suggestions on page 5. If you do use charcoal lighter fluid (and I do not recommend it), *never* squirt it onto an ignited fire. Don't even think about using gasoline, kerosene, or any other volatile fluids to light your charcoal fire. They can explode.

■ If you must use instant-light briquettes (and I do not recommend them), never use them in combination with any other starter—electric, chimney, lighting fluid, or solid starters.

- Never use an electric fire starter in the rain or while standing on wet ground.

- To prevent flare-ups, don't cook fatty food like unskinned chicken directly over the coals. The melting fat will drip onto the coals, creating flare-ups. If a flare-up occurs, move the food to the cooler parts of the grill around the perimeter of the grate, where it will drip around, but not directly over, the coals. Cover the grill tightly, and the flare-up will probably burn out by itself.

- To put out stubborn flare-ups, first cut off the oxygen supply by closing the air vents and tightly closing the lid. If you must extinguish a flare-up with a squirt of water from a spray bottle, remove the food from the grill with long-handled tongs, or the wet ashes could splatter onto the food. Put out serious grease fires with baking soda.

- If possible, allow the coals to burn out by themselves—this will take 48 hours.

- If you must dispose of coals before they are completely cool, empty them onto heavy-duty aluminum foil and soak them well in water.

- Wrap extinguished coals in heavy-duty aluminum foil, and dispose of them in a noncombustible container. Be sure there are no other combustible materials in or near the container.

- If you are at a campsite, douse the coals completely, then cover with dirt. Never cover a hot or warm fire pit with dirt, as the dirt on the surface can heat up and burn anyone who inadvertently walks over the area. (The mother of a friend of mine ended up in the hospital when this happened to her.)

Gas Grilling Safety Tips

- Most propane cylinders hold about 20 pounds, which leaves some room for the liquid to expand. Do not ask the supplier to fill the machine more than the limit.

- Never store an LP cylinder inside. It should be kept outside, stored upright, well-removed from the gas grill itself, and someplace where the temperature won't exceed 125° F. If the gas grill is stored indoors (especially during the winter months in cold areas), the cylinder must be disconnected and stored outside.

■   Every time you connect the LP cylinder to the grill, check for leaks with a soap-and-water solution. Never check for leaks with a flame.

■   Don't use the LP cylinder if it shows any external signs of damage—dents, bulges, gouges, fire damage, corrosion, leakage, or excessive rust. Take the damaged cylinder to your supplier and have it checked. Cylinders are not very expensive, and it may be easiest and safest to just buy a new one.

■   After any storage period (for example, the first time you fire up the grill after a winter hiatus), check the gas grill for leaks, deterioration, proper assembly, and burner obstructions before using. Pay special attention to the hose, which should not show any signs of abrasion, wear, or leakage. If necessary, replace it using a parts replacement kit. Always turn off the gas before inspecting any parts.

■   When lighting a gas grill, leave the lid open to prevent the gas from building up and causing an explosion.

■   If a burner doesn't ignite, turn off the gas. Leave the lid open and wait for five minutes before trying to light it again. If the burners go out during cooking (usually from a breeze blowing them out), turn off the gas, open the lid, and wait five minutes before relighting.

Appetizers, Salsas, and Dips

Grilled Focaccia with
Tomato and Mozzarella Salad

Makes 8 appetizer servings or 4 main-course servings

Focaccia is almost the same thing as pizza, but it's usually baked with just a sprinkle of herbs and served as a bread. It's fun to grill the rounds of dough, which gives them tasty brown grill marks. You can cut the salad-topped focaccia into wedges and serve it as an appetizer, or place them on a plate and serve one focaccia per person as a main course.

TOMATO AND MOZZARELLA SALAD

1 tablespoon red wine vinegar
1 garlic clove, crushed through a press
$\frac{1}{4}$ teaspoon salt
$\frac{1}{8}$ teaspoon freshly ground black pepper
3 tablespoons olive oil
1 pound plum tomatoes, cut into $\frac{1}{4}$-inch dice
4 ounces mozzarella, cut into $\frac{1}{4}$-inch dice
$\frac{1}{3}$ cup pitted and chopped brine-cured black olives
2 tablespoons chopped fresh basil

2 pounds frozen pizza or bread dough, thawed
2 tablespoons olive oil

I. To make the salad, whisk together the vinegar, garlic, salt, and pepper in a medium bowl. Whisk in the oil. Add the tomatoes, mozzarella, olives, and basil and mix. Cover and let stand at room temperature until ready to serve, up to 2 hours. Do not refrigerate.

2. To make the focaccia, build a charcoal fire in an outdoor grill and let burn down until medium-hot. You should be able to hold your hand just above grate level for 3 seconds. **IN A GAS GRILL,** preheat on High, then reduce the heat to Medium.

3. Cut the dough into four pieces, form into balls, and cover loosely with plastic wrap. On a lightly floured work surface, keeping the remaining balls covered, roll out one piece of dough into an 8-inch round. (If the dough is stubborn, pick up the round and pull and stretch it into shape.) Place on a lightly oiled piece of wax paper, brush the top with oil, and cover loosely with plastic wrap. Repeat with the other balls of dough.

4. Lightly oil the cooking grate. Flip the dough rounds onto the grill, discarding the wax paper. Cover and grill until the undersides are golden brown, about 3 minutes. Brush with oil, flip, and continue grilling until the other sides are browned and the dough is cooked through, 3 to 4 minutes more.

5. To serve, cut the focaccias into quarters and place on a serving platter. Top each wedge with a large spoonful of salad. Serve immediately.

Bruschetta with Tomatoes

Makes 8 to 12 servings

Bruschetta is one of the easiest and best ways to grill up an appetizer. It's simply bread slices brushed with olive oil, grilled, and served with the cook's choice of topping. The classic version calls for the grilled bread to be rubbed with raw garlic cloves, then crowned with a heap of chopped tomatoes. The success of the bruschetta depends on the quality of the bread and oil, so it's important to use a crusty loaf from a good bakery and high-quality olive oil. (Bread comes in many shapes and sizes, so you may have to cut large, wide slices into more manageable portions.) Make this bruschetta when your local tomatoes are at the peak of the season, ripe and full of flavor. Salting the tomatoes is a detail that makes a difference—it drains off some of the juice and enhances the flavor of the tomato flesh.

There are many bruschetta topping possibilities beyond tomatoes—try Grilled Red Peppers with Balsamic Vinegar and Garlic (page 50) or Italian Green Herb Sauce (page 72). If it can be spread, sprinkled, or slathered onto toast, it can be bruschetta.

> 2 large beefsteak tomatoes
> $1/4$ teaspoon salt
> 36 ($1/4$-inch-thick) slices crusty French or Italian bread
> $1/4$ cup olive oil, preferably extra-virgin
> 3 whole, peeled garlic cloves
> 2 tablespoons chopped fresh basil

1. Cut each tomato in half horizontally. Squeeze gently to remove most of the seeds. Cut the tomatoes into $1/2$-inch dice. Place in a colander over a bowl and sprinkle with the salt. Let the tomatoes drain for 30 minutes. Transfer to a bowl and let stand at room temperature until ready to serve, up to 2 hours. Do not refrigerate.

2. Build a charcoal fire in an outdoor grill and let burn until covered with white ash. **IN A GAS GRILL,** preheat on High.

3. Lightly brush the bread slices with the oil. Grill the bread, turning once, until lightly toasted, about 3 minutes. Lightly rub the bread slices with the garlic cloves—the rough surface of the bread will "grate" the garlic onto the bread. Don't overdo the garlic unless you are really a garlic lover.

4. Stir the basil leaves into the tomatoes. Top each bread slice with some tomatoes and serve immediately.

Black Bean and Bacon Dip
with Baked Tortilla Chips

Makes 6 to 8 servings

Sure, you can buy black bean dip, but nothing beats the homemade version. It will thicken upon standing, so thin it with a little stock, if you need to. I like to make my own tortilla chips, baked in the oven.

TORTILLA CHIPS

Eight 6-inch corn tortillas, cut into sixths
Nonstick vegetable spray

DIP

1 tablespoon vegetable oil
4 slices pork or turkey bacon
1 medium onion, chopped
1 jalapeño pepper, seeded and minced
1 garlic clove, minced
3 plum tomatoes, seeded and chopped
1 teaspoon dried oregano
$\frac{1}{2}$ teaspoon ground cumin
One 19-ounce can black beans, drained and rinsed
$\frac{1}{3}$ cup canned low-sodium chicken broth, fat removed
Salt

1. To make the chips, position racks in the center and top third of the oven and preheat to 400° F. Spread the tortilla wedges on 2 baking sheets. Spray the tortillas lightly with the nonstick spray. Bake, stirring occasionally, and switching the positions of the sheets from top to bottom halfway through baking, 10 to 12 minutes, until crisp and lightly toasted. Cool completely. Store in a paper bag at room temperature for up to 8 hours.

2. To make the dip, heat the oil in a large nonstick skillet over medium heat. Add the bacon and cook until crisp, about 5 minutes. Using tongs, transfer to paper towels and cool. Crumble the bacon and set aside.

3. Add the onion, jalapeño, and garlic to the fat in the skillet. Cook, stirring often, until the onion softens, about 4 minutes. Add the tomatoes, oregano, and cumin. Cook, stirring often, until the tomatoes soften, about 5 minutes. Stir in the beans and bacon and cook, stirring often, until the beans are hot, about 5 minutes.

4. Add the chicken broth. Using a potato masher or a slotted spoon, coarsely mash the beans. Season to taste with the salt. Serve warm, or cool to room temperature. (The dip can be prepared up to 1 day ahead, cooled, covered, and refrigerated. Thin to dipping consistency with additional broth.)

Layered Black Bean and Salsa Dip

Makes 8 to 10 servings

Serve this with *plenty* of tortilla chips, either store-bought or your own home-baked version (see preceding recipe).

> Black Bean and Bacon Dip (page 24)
> $\frac{1}{2}$ cup sour cream
> 1 ripe Haas avocado, pitted, peeled, and sliced
> Green and Red Salsa (page 28) or Summer Vegetable Salsa (page 29)
> Tortilla chips

Spread the black bean dip in a thick layer on a serving plate. Spread with the sour cream, then top with the avocado slices. Top with the salsa. Serve immediately, with the chips. (The dish can be prepared up to 4 hours ahead, covered and refrigerated.)

Guaca-Salsa-Mole

Makes about 2 cups

It is guacamole, or is it salsa? Don't worry about the name, and serve it as a dip or with fajitas (page 118).

1 large ripe beefsteak tomato, seeded and chopped into $\frac{1}{2}$-inch cubes
1 ripe Hass avocado, pitted, peeled, and chopped into $\frac{1}{2}$-inch cubes
$\frac{1}{2}$ cup sour cream, regular or reduced-fat
1 jalapeño pepper, seeded and minced
2 tablespoons minced red onion
2 tablespoons fresh lime juice
1 garlic clove, crushed through a press
$\frac{1}{4}$ teaspoon salt

Combine all of the ingredients in a large bowl. Press plastic wrap directly onto the top of the dip so it isn't exposed to any air. Refrigerate until chilled, at least 1 hour. Serve chilled.

Antipasti "Salsa"

Makes about 3 cups

This chunky "salsa" takes many of the flavors of an Italian antipasti platter and mixes them up into a great condiment for spreading onto bruschetta or crackers. Try to make it a day ahead so the flavors can blend.

> One 9-ounce package frozen artichoke hearts, thawed
> 1 large red pepper, roasted, seeded, and chopped (see Note)
> 2 medium celery ribs with leaves, finely chopped
> $\frac{1}{4}$ cup olive oil, preferably extra-virgin
> $1\frac{1}{2}$ tablespoons red wine vinegar
> 2 tablespoons chopped fresh basil
> 1 garlic clove, crushed through a press
> $\frac{1}{4}$ teaspoon salt
> $\frac{1}{8}$ teaspoon hot red pepper flakes

Mix together the artichoke hearts, red pepper, celery, oil, vinegar, basil, garlic, salt, and red pepper flakes in a medium bowl. Cover and refrigerate for at least 2 hours, or overnight.

Note To roast a pepper on the grill, see page 50. If you prefer, the pepper can be roasted under the broiler. Position a broiler rack about 6 inches from the source of heat and preheat the broiler. Broil the pepper, turning occasionally, until blackened and blistered all over, 8 to 12 minutes. Transfer the pepper to a paper bag, close the bag, and let stand for 20 minutes to cool and soften the peppers. Use a small sharp knife to remove the blackened skin.

Green and Red Salsa

FIREFIGHTER BRIAN "BARNEY" PERICONE ▪ LINDEN FIRE DEPARTMENT ▪ LINDEN, NEW JERSEY

Makes about 2 cups

Tomatillos, a staple of Mexican cooking, are becoming more readily available at supermarkets and can almost always be found in Latin groceries. They look like small green tomatoes surrounded by a papery husk (they are actually more closely related to the gooseberry than to the tomato!). If you can't find them, use a total of 12 ounces plum tomatoes, and call this "Red and Red Salsa."

8 ounces fresh tomatillos, husked and cut into $\frac{1}{2}$-inch dice
4 ounces ripe plum tomatoes, cut into $\frac{1}{2}$-inch dice
$\frac{1}{3}$ cup finely chopped red onion
$\frac{1}{4}$ cup fresh lime juice
3 tablespoons chopped fresh cilantro
4 garlic cloves, minced
1 jalapeño pepper, seeded and minced
1 teaspoon dried oregano
$\frac{1}{2}$ teaspoon ground cumin
$\frac{1}{2}$ teaspoon salt

Combine all of the ingredients in a medium glass bowl. Cover and refrigerate until chilled, at least 2 hours. Remove from the refrigerator 30 minutes before serving.

Summer Vegetable Salsa

Makes about 2¹/₂ cups

This multicolored salsa is not only a tortilla chip's best friend, but it is also great alongside just about any simply grilled fish, poultry, or meat you care to serve it with.

> 1 medium zucchini, cut into ¹/₄-inch dice
> ¹/₂ teaspoon salt, plus more to taste
> 8 ounces plum tomatoes, cut into ¹/₄-inch dice
> ¹/₂ cup cooked corn kernels, preferably from grilled corn (page 51)
> 2 tablespoons fresh lime juice
> 2 tablespoons minced red onion
> 1 jalapeño pepper, seeded and minced
> 1 garlic clove, crushed through a press

1. In a colander set over a bowl, toss the zucchini with ¹/₂ teaspoon salt. Let stand until the zucchini gives off its juices, about 30 minutes. Rinse well under cold water. A handful at a time, squeeze the excess liquid out of the zucchini and place the zucchini in a medium bowl.

2. Add the tomatoes, corn, lime juice, onion, jalapeño, and garlic. Toss and add salt to taste. Cover and refrigerate to blend the flavors, at least 1 hour. Serve chilled.

Mango-Jalapeño Salsa

This salsa is good with grilled pork chops, chicken breast, and swordfish or tuna steaks. Serve the salsa within 4 hours of making, so the flavors stay fresh.

1 ripe mango, pitted, peeled, and cut into $^{1}/_{2}$-inch cubes (see page 205)
1 jalapeño pepper, seeded and minced
2 tablespoons finely chopped red onion
2 tablespoons chopped fresh mint or cilantro
2 tablespoons fresh lime juice
Salt to taste

In a medium bowl, mix the mango, jalapeño, red onion, mint, and lime juice. Season with salt, to taste. Cover and refrigerate until chilled, about 1 hour.

Salads and

Sides

Beet, Fennel, and Orange Salad

Makes 6 servings

Ruby-red, this salad is packed with interesting flavors and textures. Don't re-frigerate it for too long—it's best if each main ingredient keeps some of its distinctive flavor and color. I give instructions for roasting the beets on the grill, but they can be baked in a 400° F oven for about 1 hour.

4 medium beets ($1\frac{1}{4}$ pounds)
1 medium (10-ounce) fennel bulb, base trimmed
3 medium seedless oranges, peeled and cut into $\frac{1}{4}$-inch-thick rounds
1 small red onion, thinly sliced
2 tablespoons balsamic vinegar
Zest of 1 orange
$\frac{1}{4}$ teaspoon salt
$\frac{1}{4}$ teaspoon freshly ground black pepper
$\frac{1}{4}$ cup olive oil

1. Build a charcoal fire in an outdoor grill and let burn until covered with white ash. Do not spread out the coals, but leave them heaped in a mound in the center of the grill. **IN A GAS GRILL,** preheat on High, then reduce the heat to Medium.

2. Wrap the beets in foil. Place the beets on the cooler, outer perimeter of the cooking grate, not directly over the coals. Cover the grill and roast the beets un-til tender, about 1 hour. **IN A GAS GRILL,** place on the grate and cook for 1 hour, turning occasionally. Cool the beets completely. Peel, then slice into $\frac{1}{2}$-inch rounds. Place in a medium bowl.

3. Trim the feathery green tops from the fennel. Chop the fennel tops and re-serve 2 tablespoons. (If the fennel does not have tops attached, substitute 2 ta-blespoons fresh tarragon or parsley.) Trim the base of the bulb and discard the outer layer. Cut the fennel in half lengthwise and cut out the thick core. Thinly slice the fennel crosswise. Add the oranges, red onion, sliced fennel, and fennel tops to the beets.

4. In a small bowl, whisk together the vinegar, orange zest, salt, and pepper. Gradually whisk in the oil. Pour over the salad and toss. Cover and refrigerate until chilled, at least 1 hour, and up to 3 hours. Serve chilled.

Old-Fashioned Cole Slaw

Makes 6 to 8 servings

The hardest part about making slaw is slicing the cabbage. If you have a food processor, use the thinnest slicing blade (not the shredding blade) to do the work.

> 1 cup mayonnaise, regular or reduced-fat
> $\frac{1}{4}$ cup milk
> 1 tablespoon cider vinegar
> 1 teaspoon Dijon mustard
> $\frac{1}{2}$ teaspoon celery seeds
> $\frac{1}{4}$ teaspoon salt
> $\frac{1}{4}$ teaspoon freshly ground black pepper
> 12 ounces green cabbage (about $\frac{1}{2}$ medium head),
>   cored and thinly sliced
> 1 medium red bell pepper, seeded and thinly sliced
> 1 medium carrot, shredded
> 1 small onion, grated into a pulp on the large holes of a box grater

1. In a large bowl, whisk together the mayonnaise, milk, vinegar, mustard, celery seed, salt, and pepper.

2. Add the cabbage, red pepper, carrot, and onion and mix well. Cover and refrigerate until ready to serve, at least 2 hours. Serve chilled.

Napa Cabbage and Pineapple Slaw

FIREFIGHTER VAUGHN MILLER ▪ **VENTURA COUNTY FIRE DEPARTMENT** ▪
VENTURA, CALIFORNIA

Makes 4 to 6 servings

A California native, Vaughn serves this salad with Asian-flavored grilled foods. It's an unusual blend of ingredients that really hits the spot.

3 tablespoons rice vinegar
$\frac{1}{2}$ teaspoon salt
$\frac{1}{2}$ cup vegetable oil
1 tablespoon dark Asian sesame oil
4 cups thinly shredded Napa cabbage (8 ounces)
$\frac{1}{2}$ medium pineapple, peeled, cored, and cut into $\frac{1}{2}$-inch cubes
    (about 2 cups)
1 medium red bell pepper, seeded and thinly sliced
2 scallions, white and green parts, chopped
1 jalapeño pepper, seeded and minced
$\frac{1}{3}$ cup chopped fresh cilantro

1. In a large bowl, whisk together the rice vinegar and salt. Gradually whisk in the vegetable oil and sesame oil.

2. Add the cabbage, pineapple, red pepper, scallions, and jalapeño and toss well. Cover and refrigerate until chilled, at least 1 hour. Just before serving, stir in the cilantro. Serve chilled.

Gazpacho Salad

Make this in a glass bowl so everyone can see the colorful layers of vegetables and compliment you on your artistic talents. When they taste it, they'll also compliment you on your cooking skills.

> 3 cups ($\frac{1}{2}$-inch cubes) Italian or French bread cubes, with crusts
> $\frac{2}{3}$ cup plus 3 tablespoons olive oil
> 3 tablespoons red wine vinegar
> $\frac{1}{4}$ teaspoon salt
> $\frac{1}{4}$ teaspoon freshly ground black pepper
> 3 pickling (Kirby) cucumbers, scrubbed but unpeeled, cut into
> $\frac{1}{2}$-inch cubes (2 cups)
> $1\frac{1}{2}$ pounds plum tomatoes, cut into $\frac{1}{2}$-inch cubes
> $\frac{1}{2}$ cup thinly sliced scallions (white and green parts)
> 1 large Italian frying (Cubanelle) pepper, or 1 small green bell pepper,
>   seeded and chopped

1. Position a rack in the top third of the oven and preheat to 400° F. In a large roasting pan, toss the bread cubes with 3 tablespoons of the oil. Bake, tossing occasionally, until golden brown, about 10 minutes. Cool completely.

2. In a medium bowl, whisk together the vinegar, salt, and pepper. Gradually whisk in the remaining $\frac{2}{3}$ cup oil. Set the dressing aside.

3. In a large glass bowl, layer the cucumbers, then the tomatoes, scallions, and pepper. Top with the bread cubes. Cover and refrigerate until chilled, at least 1 hour, and up to 4 hours.

4. To serve, toss the salad, gradually adding the dressing. Serve immediately.

Pepperoni Pasta Salad

FIREFIGHTER JOE BRUNI ▪ ST. PETERSBURG FIRE DEPARTMENT ▪ ST. PETERSBURG, FLORIDA

Makes 8 servings

Joe's pasta salad has more vegetables than a salad bar, plus the added attraction of pepperoni.

ITALIAN DRESSING

3 tablespoons red wine vinegar

1 tablespoon Dijon mustard

$^1/_2$ teaspoon dried oregano

1 garlic clove, crushed through a press

$^1/_2$ teaspoon salt, plus more to taste

$^1/_4$ teaspoon freshly ground black pepper, plus more to taste

$^1/_2$ cup olive oil

8 ounces rotini pasta

One 15$^1/_2$-ounce can kidney beans, rinsed and drained

4 ounces thinly sliced pepperoni

1 small red onion, finely chopped

$^1/_2$ pint cherry tomatoes, cut in half

1 cup frozen peas, thawed

1 cup thinly sliced mushrooms

1 medium carrot, shredded

$^1/_4$ cup thinly sliced California black olives

I. To make the dressing, whisk together the vinegar, mustard, oregano, garlic, $^1/_2$ teaspoon salt, and $^1/_4$ teaspoon pepper in a small bowl. Gradually whisk in the oil. Set the dressing aside.

2. Bring a large pot of lightly salted water to a boil over high heat. Add the pasta and cook until tender, about 9 minutes, or according to the package directions. Drain, rinse under cold water until completely cooled, and drain well. Transfer to a large bowl.

3. Add the dressing, kidney beans, pepperoni, onion, cherry tomatoes, peas, mushrooms, carrot, and olives. Toss well. Cover and refrigerate until chilled, at least 1 hour. Season with additional salt and pepper to taste before serving.

Garden Pasta Salad with Lemon Dressing

Makes 8 servings

Everyone loves pasta salad. This one features summer vegetables, including tomatoes and zucchini, in a simple lemon dressing. Pasta salads soak up their dressing and change flavor as they stand, so it's a good idea to dress the salad with some reserved dressing just before serving.

> $^{1}/_{4}$ cup fresh lemon juice
> 1 teaspoon dried oregano
> 1 garlic clove, crushed through a press
> $^{1}/_{4}$ teaspoon salt, plus more to taste
> $^{1}/_{4}$ teaspoon freshly ground black pepper, plus more to taste
> $^{3}/_{4}$ cup olive oil
> 1 pound small pasta shells
> 4 ripe medium plum tomatoes, seeded and chopped into $^{1}/_{4}$-inch pieces
> 1 medium zucchini, cut into thin rounds
> 2 medium celery ribs, cut into $^{1}/_{8}$-inch-thick slices
> 3 scallions, white and green parts, finely chopped
> 3 tablespoons chopped fresh basil

1. In a medium bowl, whisk together the lemon juice, oregano, garlic, $^{1}/_{4}$ teaspoon salt, and $^{1}/_{4}$ teaspoon pepper until combined. Gradually whisk in the oil. Set the dressing aside.

2. Bring a large pot of lightly salted water to a boil over high heat. Add the pasta and cook until tender, about 4 minutes or according to the package directions. Drain, rinse under cold water until completely cooled, and drain well. Transfer to a large bowl.

3. Add the tomatoes, zucchini, celery, and scallions. Add half of the dressing and toss well. Cover and refrigerate for at least 1 hour, or up to 1 day. Just before serving, add the basil and the remaining dressing and toss again. Season with additional salt and pepper. Serve chilled or at room temperature.

Potato Salad, Italian-Style

Makes 6 servings

If you ask an Italian *nonna* to make her famous recipe for potato salad, it will be pretty different from an American grandma's version. Both are great, but sometimes a noncreamy potato salad will best complement the rest of the menu—especially when you're serving Mediterranean foods. Normally, *nonna*'s dressing would use plenty of olive oil, but I substitute chicken broth for some of it, and it works beautifully.

3 pounds red-skinned potatoes, scrubbed but unpeeled
2 medium celery ribs with leaves, chopped
1 medium Italian frying (Cubanelle) pepper, or 1 small green bell
    pepper, seeded and chopped
$^1/_3$ cup minced red onion
3 tablespoons bottled capers, drained, rinsed, and chopped if large

DRESSING

2 tablespoons red wine vinegar, plus more to taste
4 anchovy fillets in oil, drained and minced into a paste, or 1 teaspoon
    anchovy paste
1 garlic clove, crushed under a knife
$^1/_4$ teaspoon salt, plus more to taste
$^1/_4$ teaspoon freshly ground black pepper, plus more to taste
$^1/_2$ cup canned low-sodium chicken broth, fat removed
2 tablespoons olive oil
2 tablespoons chopped fresh basil

1. Bring a large pot of lightly salted water to a boil over high heat. Add the potatoes and cook until just tender, 20 to 25 minutes. Drain and rinse under cold running water until cool enough to handle. If you wish, peel the potatoes (I don't). Slice into thick rounds into a medium bowl. Add the celery, frying pepper, red onion, and capers.

continued

2. To make the dressing, combine the vinegar, anchovies, garlic, $1/4$ teaspoon salt, and $1/4$ teaspoon pepper in a blender. With the machine running, add the broth, then the oil. Pour over the salad and mix well.

3. Cover and refrigerate until chilled, at least 2 hours. Before serving, taste and season as needed with additional vinegar, salt, and pepper. Stir in the basil. Serve chilled.

New Potato and Green Bean Salad with Spiced Yogurt Dressing

FIREFIGHTER STEVEN FERNANDES ▪ LINDEN FIRE DEPARTMENT ▪ LINDEN, NEW JERSEY

Makes 8 to 12 servings

Steve has always promoted good, healthy cooking in his firehouse. Combined with Indian spices like cumin and mustard seed, yogurt can become a tangy potato salad dressing. Use low-fat mayonnaise, if you wish.

3 pounds small new potatoes, scrubbed
$1/2$ pound green beans, trimmed and cut into 1-inch lengths
2 tablespoons vegetable oil
1 teaspoon cumin seeds
1 teaspoon yellow mustard seeds
$2/3$ cup plain low-fat yogurt
$2/3$ cup mayonnaise, regular or reduced-fat
6 scallions (white and green parts), finely chopped
$1/2$ teaspoon salt
$1/4$ teaspoon freshly ground black pepper
$1/8$ teaspoon cayenne pepper

1. Bring a large pot of lightly salted water to a boil over high heat. Add the potatoes and cook until just tender, 20 to 25 minutes. During the last 2 minutes, add the green beans and cook until the green beans are crisp-tender and done at the same time as the potatoes. (Or, cook the green beans in a separate saucepan.) Drain and rinse under cold running water until cool enough to handle. If desired, peel, then cut the potatoes into thick slices. Place in a large bowl.

2. In a small dry skillet, toast the cumin and mustard seeds over medium heat, stirring constantly, until fragrant and starting to pop, about 2 minutes. Immediately transfer to a plate to cool.

3. In a medium bowl, fold together the yogurt, mayonnaise, cooled seeds, scallions, salt, and black and cayenne peppers. Do not whisk. Pour the dressing over the vegetables and fold together. Cover and refrigerate until chilled, at least 2 hours. Serve chilled.

Picnic Potato Salad

Makes 6 to 8 servings

It's a tough call to give a recipe for classic creamy potato salad, because everyone has such strong feelings about it—usually based on the memory of Mom's or Grandma's version. For my money, this is a good place to start, and you can tweak it to suit yourself. Some people like to make potato salad with Idaho potatoes, which break up more than the red-skinned variety. If you are using thin-skinned red or white potatoes, you can leave them unpeeled, but brown Idaho's must be peeled. For a slightly sweet potato salad, stir in 2 tablespoons sweet pickle relish, or use sandwich spread instead of mayonnaise.

> 3 pounds red- or white-skinned potatoes, scrubbed
> $^3/_4$ cup mayonnaise
> $^1/_2$ cup sour cream
> 1 tablespoon Dijon mustard
> 2 tablespoons cider vinegar
> 4 hard-cooked eggs, chopped
> 2 medium celery ribs with leaves, chopped
> 3 scallions, white and green parts, chopped
> $^1/_4$ teaspoon salt
> $^1/_4$ teaspoon freshly ground black pepper

1. Bring a large pot of lightly salted water to a boil over high heat. Add the potatoes and cook until just tender, about 20 to 25 minutes. Drain and rinse under cold running water until cool enough to handle. If desired, peel the potatoes.

2. In a large bowl, whisk together the mayonnaise, sour cream, and mustard. Cut the potatoes into thick rounds and add to the bowl. Sprinkle the potatoes with the vinegar. Add the eggs, celery, and scallions and mix well. Season with the salt and pepper. Cover and refrigerate until chilled, at least 2 hours. Serve chilled.

Brown Rice and Black Bean Salad

FIREFIGHTER VICKIE WOLF ▪ REDDING FIRE DEPARTMENT ▪ REDDING, CALIFORNIA

Makes 8 servings

This colorful salad would be welcome on any picnic table as a side dish. But, it is so rib-sticking you may want to serve it as a cool summer lunch. Rice gets unappetizingly hard if served chilled, so remove the salad from the refrigerator at least 30 minutes before serving.

3 tablespoons cider vinegar
1 garlic clove, crushed through a press
1 teaspoon salt
$\frac{1}{4}$ teaspoon freshly ground black pepper
$\frac{1}{2}$ cup olive oil
1 cup brown rice
One 15-ounce can black beans, drained and rinsed
2 medium tomatoes, cut into $\frac{1}{2}$-inch dice
2 medium celery ribs, cut into $\frac{1}{4}$-inch-thick slices
2 scallions, white and green parts, thinly sliced
2 tablespoons chopped fresh oregano, basil, or parsley
6 ounces crumbled feta cheese

1. To make the dressing, whisk together the vinegar, garlic, $\frac{1}{2}$ teaspoon of the salt, and pepper in a medium bowl. Gradually whisk in the oil. Set aside.

2. In a medium saucepan, combine the brown rice, $2\frac{1}{2}$ cups water, and the remaining $\frac{1}{2}$ teaspoon salt. Bring to a boil over high heat. Reduce the heat to low and cover. Cook until the rice is tender and has absorbed the liquid, about 45 minutes. Place in a large bowl and cool completely.

3. Add the black beans, tomatoes, celery, scallions, fresh herbs, and feta cheese to the rice. Stir in the dressing. Serve immediately, or cover and refrigerate for up to 8 hours. If making ahead, remove from the refrigerator 30 minutes before serving.

Creamy Tomato and Corn Salad

Makes 4 to 6 servings

When August rolls around, I know firefighters who say they could eat corn and tomatoes for breakfast, lunch, and dinner. To cut corn from the cob, slice off the base of the corn so it will stand steady and not rock. Stand the ear of corn on end, and slice downward, removing the corn kernels where they meet the cob. You will get about $^1/_2$ cup corn from a medium-sized ear.

6 tablespoons plain low-fat yogurt
2 tablespoons olive oil
1 tablespoon red wine vinegar
1 teaspoon chili powder
$^1/_4$ teaspoon salt
3 cups cooked corn kernels, preferably grilled (see page 51)
4 scallions, white and green parts, chopped
2 tablespoons chopped fresh oregano or basil
3 ripe medium beefsteak tomatoes (1 pound), cut into 1-inch cubes

1. In a large bowl, stir the yogurt, oil, vinegar, chili powder, and salt until well mixed.

2. Add the corn, scallions, and oregano. Stir well. Cover and refrigerate until chilled, at least 1 hour. Just before serving, stir in the tomatoes.

Easy Baked Beans

Makes about 12 servings

Next time you have to bring a warm dish to a big firehouse picnic, bring a big pot of these baked beans.

> 1 tablespoon vegetable oil
> 4 strips pork or turkey bacon
> 1 large onion, chopped
> One 12-ounce can lager beer
> $\frac{1}{3}$ cup ketchup
> $\frac{1}{3}$ cup honey
> 3 tablespoons spicy brown mustard
> Four 15-ounce cans white kidney (cannellini) beans, drained and rinsed

1. Position a rack in the center of the oven and preheat to 350° F. In a Dutch oven or flameproof casserole, heat the oil over medium heat. Add the bacon and cook until crisp, about 5 minutes. Using tongs, transfer the bacon to paper towels to cool. Crumble the bacon and set aside.

2. Add the onion to the fat in the Dutch oven and cook, stirring occasionally, until golden brown, about 6 minutes. Stir in the beer, ketchup, honey, and brown mustard. Stir in the beans and reserved bacon. Bring to a simmer.

3. Cover and bake for 1 hour. Uncover and continue baking until the beans have absorbed most of the liquid and look glazed, about 30 minutes. Serve hot.

Grilled Asparagus
with Orange-Olive Dressing

Makes 4 to 6 servings

I know people who have made an entire meal of these grilled asparagus spears. The exact cooking time depends on the thickness of the asparagus.

> 1 tablespoon fresh lemon juice
> Grated zest of 1 orange
> $\frac{1}{8}$ teaspoon salt
> $\frac{1}{8}$ teaspoon freshly ground black pepper
> $\frac{1}{4}$ cup olive oil, preferably extra-virgin
> $1\frac{1}{2}$ pounds pencil-thin asparagus, woody stems discarded
> $\frac{1}{4}$ cup pitted and finely chopped black brine-cured olives

1. Build a charcoal fire in an outdoor grill and let burn until covered with white ash. **IN A GAS GRILL,** preheat on High.

2. In a small bowl, whisk together the lemon juice, orange zest, salt, and pepper. Gradually whisk in the oil. Toss the asparagus and dressing in a zippered plastic bag, but don't marinate the asparagus.

3. Lightly oil the cooking grate. Place the asparagus on the grill, perpendicular to the grill grid, reserving the dressing. Grill, turning occasionally, until the asparagus is tender, about 5 minutes. Transfer to a serving plate. Stir the olives into the dressing and spoon over the asparagus. Serve immediately.

Bruce's Grilled Parmesan Zucchini

BRUCE KOKE • BLOOMINGTON, MINNESOTA

Makes 4 to 6 servings

You'll find lots of ways to serve Bruce's grilled zucchini—as a side dish, as part of a grilled vegetable platter, or even as a warm salad. Sometimes I vary it by adding some grilled plum tomato halves, too.

> 2 tablespoons red wine vinegar
> $\frac{1}{2}$ teaspoon dried Italian seasoning
> 1 garlic clove, crushed through a press
> $\frac{1}{4}$ teaspoon salt
> $\frac{1}{4}$ teaspoon freshly ground black pepper
> $\frac{1}{2}$ cup olive oil, preferably extra-virgin
> 4 small zucchini, scrubbed and quartered lengthwise
> $\frac{1}{3}$ cup freshly grated Parmesan cheese

1. In a small bowl, whisk together the vinegar, Italian seasoning, garlic, salt, and pepper. Gradually whisk in the oil. Place the zucchini and marinade in a zippered plastic bag. Seal the bag and let stand at room temperature for 1 hour.

2. Build a charcoal fire in an outdoor grill and let burn until the coals are covered with white ash. **IN A GAS GRILL,** preheat on High.

3. Lightly oil the cooking grate. Place the zucchini on the grill, running perpendicular to the grill grid. Grill, turning occasionally, until browned and tender, about 8 minutes. Transfer to a serving bowl and sprinkle with the cheese. Serve hot.

Grilled New Potatoes
with Mustard-Soy Glaze

Makes 4 to 6 servings

Whenever I serve these potatoes, people are surprised to find that they've been grilled—I guess everyone expects their grilled potatoes to be wrapped in foil. Once you've made them, it will be hard to go back to plain old foiled potatoes.

1$\frac{1}{2}$ pounds small new potatoes, scrubbed but unpeeled (if using larger
   potatoes, cut into 1-inch chunks)
2 tablespoons Dijon mustard
2 tablespoons soy sauce
2 tablespoons olive oil
$\frac{1}{4}$ teaspoon salt, plus more to taste
$\frac{1}{4}$ teaspoon freshly ground black pepper

1. Place the potatoes in a large pot and add enough cold water to cover by 1 inch. Bring to a boil over high heat. Add salt to taste. Cook until the potatoes are barely tender when pierced with the tip of a knife (they will cook further on the grill), about 20 minutes, depending on their size. Drain and rinse under cold running water until cool enough to handle. Cut each potato in half.

2. In a medium bowl, whisk together the mustard, soy sauce, oil, $\frac{1}{4}$ teaspoon salt, and pepper until smooth. Add the potatoes and toss gently to coat them with the sauce. Let stand at room temperature for 1 hour.

3. Build a charcoal fire in an outdoor grill and let burn until covered with white ash. **IN A GAS GRILL,** preheat on High.

4. Lightly oil the cooking grate. Place the potatoes on the grill and cover. Grill, occasionally turning the potatoes and basting with the marinade, until browned and tender, about 10 minutes. Transfer to a serving bowl and serve immediately.

"Big Daddy's" Grilled Portobello Mushrooms

CHRISTOPHER "BIG DADDY" LUKENDA ▪ LINDEN, NEW JERSEY

Makes 6 servings

"Big Daddy" likes big mushrooms, and portobellos are about as big as they get. His shallot and garlic baste is big on flavor, too.

$\frac{1}{3}$ cup olive oil, preferably extra-virgin
2 tablespoons chopped shallots
2 garlic cloves, minced
6 large portobello mushrooms
$\frac{1}{4}$ teaspoon salt
$\frac{1}{4}$ teaspoon freshly ground black pepper

1. In a small saucepan, heat the oil, shallots, and garlic over low heat until tiny bubbles surround the vegetables. Remove from the heat and let stand for 10 minutes. Strain into a small bowl, pressing hard on the solids. Set aside.

2. Quickly rinse the mushrooms under cold water to remove any grit and wipe clean with paper towels.

3. Build a charcoal fire in an outdoor grill and let burn until covered with white ash. **IN A GAS GRILL,** preheat on High.

4. Brush the mushrooms with some of the shallot-garlic oil. Season with the salt and pepper. Lightly oil the cooking grate. Place the mushrooms on the grill and cover. Grill, occasionally turning and brushing with the oil, until tender, 10 to 15 minutes. Serve hot, drizzled with any remaining oil.

Grilled Red Peppers with Balsamic Vinegar and Garlic

Makes 6 servings

Some people grill whole red peppers, but if they are cut and opened to form a long strip, they will cook faster and have a crunchier texture. Keep in mind that the peppers should be grilled just until the skins are charred and blistered enough to remove the skins—don't burn a hole through them! Use any leftover peppers in a mozzarella sandwich on toasted Italian bread.

4 large red bell peppers
2 tablespoons balsamic vinegar
2 tablespoons olive oil, preferably extra-virgin
$\frac{1}{4}$ teaspoon salt
$\frac{1}{4}$ teaspoon freshly ground black pepper
1 garlic clove, minced
2 tablespoons chopped fresh basil

1. Cut off the top of 1 pepper and reserve. Poke out the stem and discard. Cut the bottom inch off the pepper and reserve. Slice down the side of the pepper and open it up into a long strip. Repeat with the other peppers.

2. Build a charcoal fire in an outdoor grill and let burn until covered with white ash. **IN A GAS GRILL,** preheat on High.

3. Lightly oil the cooking grate. Place the pepper strips, tops, and bottoms on the grill, skin sides down, and cover. Grill the peppers, skin sides down, until the skins are blackened and blistered, about 6 to 8 minutes. Don't worry if every single part of the skin isn't charred. Transfer the peppers to a paper bag and close the bag. Let stand for 20 minutes—the heat will soften the peppers and make the skins easier to remove. Using a sharp knife, remove the blackened skins. Don't rinse the peppers under water unless you absolutely have to.

4. In a small bowl, whisk together the vinegar, oil, salt, and pepper. Whisk in the garlic. Cut the peppers into 1-inch-wide strips. Place the peppers in a shallow dish. Drizzle with the dressing and sprinkle with the basil. Cover and refrigerate for at least 2 hours before serving. Serve chilled or at room temperature.

Grilled Corn with Basil Butter

Makes 8 servings

When you want to grill corn, don't bother shucking the ears or soaking them, and forget about wrapping the ears in foil. Just grill it over hot coals until the husks are charred. You'll probably need to wear clean gloves to remove the husks and silk, but other than that detail, this is the easiest and best way to get grilled corn on the table.

> 8 tablespoons (1 stick) unsalted butter, softened
> 3 tablespoons finely chopped fresh basil
> 8 ears fresh corn, with husks and silk intact

1. In a small bowl, mash the butter and basil. Cover and set aside at room temperature until ready to serve.

2. Build a charcoal fire in an outdoor grill and let burn until covered with white ash. **IN A GAS GRILL,** preheat on High.

3. Place the corn on the grill (there's no need to oil the grate) and cover. Grill, turning occasionally, until the husks are charred on all sides, about 15 minutes. Protecting your hands with gloves or large kitchen towels, remove the husks and silk. Serve hot, with the basil butter.

Sweet-and-Sour Onions

Makes 6 servings

Sweet and tender, these onions were made to top a grilled steak or a juicy burger. They can be prepared with Vidalia or regular yellow onions, too.

Nonstick vegetable oil spray
6 medium red onions, sliced into $\frac{1}{4}$-inch-thick rings
6 tablespoons balsamic vinegar
6 tablespoons ($\frac{3}{4}$ stick) unsalted butter
6 tablespoons light brown sugar
Salt, to taste
Freshly ground black pepper, to taste

1. Tear off six 12-inch squares of aluminum foil. Spray one side of each foil square with the nonstick spray. On the bottom third of each oiled square, place 1 sliced onion, 1 tablespoon vinegar, 1 tablespoon butter, and 1 tablespoon brown sugar. Season with the salt and pepper. Fold the foil over to enclose the onion, and roll up the open edges to make a tight seal.

2. Build a charcoal fire in an outdoor grill and let burn until covered with white ash. **IN A GAS GRILL,** preheat on High.

3. Place the foil packets on the grill and cover. Cook for 10 minutes. Move the packets to the cooler edges of the grill, not directly over the coals. **IN A GAS GRILL,** turn the burner to Medium. Cook until the onions are tender and glazed (open a packet to check), 10 to 15 minutes. Unwrap and serve the onions hot or at room temperature.

Grilled Carrots with Raspberry Glaze

Makes 4 to 6 servings

Sure, carrots can be grilled, but you have to start by choosing the right carrots. They should be long and slender, no more than 1 inch wide.

1½ pounds long, slender carrots, scrubbed but unpeeled
1 tablespoon olive oil
½ teaspoon salt
¼ teaspoon freshly ground black pepper
⅓ cup seedless raspberry preserves
1 teaspoon cornstarch
2 tablespoons balsamic vinegar

1. Bring a large pot of lightly salted water to a boil over high heat. Add the carrots and blanch for 2 minutes. Drain and rinse under cold running water. Place in a shallow dish and toss with the oil, salt, and pepper.

2. In a small saucepan, melt the preserves over low heat. Dissolve the cornstarch in the vinegar and stir into the preserves. Simmer until thickened. Set aside.

3. Build a charcoal fire in an outdoor grill and let burn until covered with white ash. **IN A GAS GRILL,** preheat on High.

4. Lightly oil the cooking grate. Place the carrots on the grill, perpendicular to the grid of the grate. Cover and grill, turning occasionally, until the carrots are crisp-tender, about 5 minutes. Reheat the glaze, if necessary to return it to a basting consistency, and continue grilling, basting with the glaze, and turning the carrots until tender and glazed, about 3 more minutes. Serve immediately.

Penne with Grilled Zucchini and Ricotta

FIREFIGHTER HERBERT PARMENTER ▪ LADDER COMPANY 152 ▪
NEW YORK FIRE DEPARTMENT ▪ NEW YORK, NEW YORK

Makes 6 to 8 side-dish or 4 to 6 main-course servings

Herbie, the computer bug (his nickname is Herbie.com), really helped me with my computer skills writing this book, and is a great help preparing meals in the kitchen. Grilled vegetables are finding their way into lots of pasta dishes lately, like this one with grilled zucchini and ricotta cheese. Tossed with a bit of the pasta cooking water, the cheese melts into a fantastic creamy sauce.

> $\frac{1}{4}$ cup olive oil
> 2 garlic cloves, crushed under a knife
> 3 medium zucchini, scrubbed and cut lengthwise into $\frac{1}{4}$-inch-thick
>   strips
> $\frac{1}{2}$ teaspoon salt
> $\frac{1}{4}$ teaspoon freshly ground black pepper, plus more to taste
> 1 pound penne
> 2 cups ricotta cheese
> $\frac{1}{2}$ cup freshly grated Parmesan cheese

1. In a small saucepan, heat the oil and garlic over low heat just until tiny bubbles surround the garlic. Remove from the heat and set aside.

2. Build a charcoal fire in an outdoor grill and let burn until covered with white ash. **IN A GAS GRILL,** preheat on High.

3. Lightly oil the cooking grate. Season the zucchini with the salt and pepper. Place the zucchini on the grill and cover. Grill, turning and basting occasionally with the garlic oil, until tender and browned, about 6 minutes. Transfer to a cutting board and cover loosely with foil to keep warm.

4. Meanwhile, bring a large pot of lightly salted water to a boil over high heat. Add the penne and cook until *al dente*, about 9 minutes, or according to the

package directions. Remove and reserve 1 cup of the cooking water. Drain the pasta and return it to the cooking pot.

5. Coarsely chop the zucchini and add to the pot. Add the ricotta and Parmesan cheeses and any remaining garlic oil. Stir, adding enough of the cooking water to make a creamy sauce. Season to taste with pepper and serve immediately.

Marinades, Rubs, and Sauces

White Wine and Herb Marinade

Makes about 1¹/₃ cups

A flavorful, all-purpose marinade, made thick with lots of herbs and grated citrus zest that cling to the food, giving it a delicious herbed crust. It is especially good made with fresh herbs. I think it's best on fish and chicken—just don't leave the fish in the marinade for too long.

> ¹/₂ cup dry white wine
> 1 tablespoon chopped fresh rosemary or 1¹/₂ teaspoons dried
> 1 tablespoon chopped fresh oregano or 1¹/₂ teaspoons dried
> 1 tablespoon chopped fresh thyme or 1¹/₂ teaspoons dried
> 1 teaspoon fennel seeds, crushed
> Grated zest of 1 lemon
> 2 garlic cloves, crushed through a press
> ¹/₂ teaspoon salt
> ¹/₂ teaspoon hot red pepper flakes
> ¹/₂ cup olive oil, preferably extra-virgin

In a medium glass or nonreactive bowl, whisk together all the ingredients, except the oil. Gradually whisk in the oil. Use immediately or cover with plastic wrap and store in the refrigerator for up to 1 day.

Tuscan Red Wine Marinade

Makes about 1¼ cups

Even though this marinade is Tuscan-inspired, don't use Italian Chianti. A good, not-too-expensive Californian red zinfandel or Merlot will do. Try it as a marinade for grilled vegetables, as well as chicken, pork, and beef.

1 cup hearty red wine
1 tablespoon chopped fresh rosemary or 1½ teaspoons dried
1 tablespoon chopped fresh sage or 1½ teaspoons dried
2 garlic cloves, minced
¼ teaspoon salt
¼ teaspoon hot red pepper flakes
⅓ cup olive oil, preferably extra-virgin

In a medium glass or nonreactive bowl, whisk together all the ingredients, except the oil. Gradually whisk in the oil. Use immediately or cover with plastic wrap and refrigerate for up to 1 day.

Zinfandel-Mint Marinade

Makes about 1½ cups

As a marinade for leg of lamb, this can't be beat. Try it another time with beef tenderloin or pork chops.

$^3/_4$ cup hearty red wine, such as zinfandel

$^1/_3$ cup chopped fresh mint or 2 tablespoons dried mint

2 scallions, white and green parts, chopped

2 tablespoons balsamic vinegar

2 tablespoons olive oil, preferably extra-virgin

2 garlic cloves, crushed through a press

$^1/_4$ teaspoon salt

$^1/_4$ teaspoon freshly ground black pepper

In a medium glass or nonreactive bowl, whisk the wine, mint, scallions, vinegar, oil, garlic, salt, and pepper. Use immediately, or cover with plastic wrap and refrigerate for up to 1 day.

Firehouse Marinade and Basting Sauce

KENT DAVID AND CHRIS BRAZZELE ▪ NAPERVILLE FIRE DEPARTMENT ▪ NAPERVILLE, ILLINOIS

Makes about 3 cups

My indirect-fire method of grilling chicken is the best, but it's certainly not the only way. Whenever a fire department throws a chicken barbecue to raise funds, the poultry is grilled directly over the coals and basted with plenty of this thick, mayonnaise-like sauce—a sure way to get flare-ups, but these cooks are professional firefighters and can take the heat. Kent and Chris sent me their version, based on a recipe developed in the 1940s at Cornell University. Use half of the mixture as a marinade and reserve the other half as a basting sauce, so the basting sauce doesn't touch any raw poultry. This makes enough for up to 6 pounds of chicken.

> 1 large egg
> 1 cup vegetable oil
> 2 cups cider vinegar
> 2 tablespoons salt, or to taste
> 1 tablespoon poultry seasoning
> $\frac{1}{2}$ teaspoon freshly ground black pepper

1. Place the uncracked egg in a small bowl and cover with hot tap water. Let stand for 5 minutes to remove the chill from the egg.

2. Crack the egg into a medium glass or nonreactive bowl. Using an electric mixer at low speed, beat the egg. Slowly beat in the oil—it should take about 1 minute to add the cup. Beat in the vinegar, salt, poultry seasoning, and pepper. Cover tightly with plastic wrap and refrigerate until ready to use, up to 1 day. Use half of the mixture as a marinade for chicken. Set the other half aside to use as a basting sauce.

Jamaican Jerk Marinade

Makes about ²/₃ cup

To make this really authentic (and properly "where's-the-fire-extin-guisher?" spicy), make it with a Scotch bonnet chile pepper. It looks like a little tam-o'-shanter—either red, yellow, or orange—and can be found in many supermarkets. If necessary, substitute a serrano or jalapeño pepper. Pork and chicken are both great when "jerked" in this marinade.

> 6 scallions, trimmed, white and green parts coarsely chopped
> ¹/₂ cup fresh lime juice
> 2 tablespoons vegetable oil
> 1 tablespoon dark rum
> 1¹/₄ teaspoons ground allspice
> 1 teaspoon dried thyme
> ¹/₂ teaspoon salt
> 1 Scotch bonnet chile pepper, seeded and chopped
> 2 garlic cloves, crushed under a knife

In a blender, combine all of the ingredients and process until smooth. Use immediately. Or, pour into an airtight glass or plastic container and refrigerate for up to 1 day.

Teriyaki Marinade

Makes I cup

Teriyaki flavors make just about any grilled food taste even better—chicken, beef, pork, turkey—even tuna and salmon steaks.

$1/4$ cup vegetable oil

3 tablespoons dark Asian sesame oil

$1/4$ cup soy sauce, preferably a Japanese brand

$1/4$ cup sweet sherry

1 tablespoon light brown sugar

1 tablespoon shredded fresh ginger (use the large holes of a box grater)

1 medium scallion, finely chopped

1 garlic clove, minced

Mix together all of the ingredients in a small bowl. Use immediately, or cover tightly with plastic wrap and refrigerate for up to 1 day.

Tandoori Marinade

Makes about 1¹/₂ cups

Spices and yogurt make an incredibly tasty Indian marinade. Most people use it for chicken, but it is great as a marinade for butterflied leg of lamb.

> 1 cup plain low-fat yogurt
> 1 small onion, coarsely chopped
> 1 tablespoon shredded fresh ginger (use the large holes of a box grater)
> 2 garlic cloves, crushed under a knife
> 1¹/₂ teaspoons ground coriander
> 1¹/₂ teaspoons ground cumin
> 1 teaspoon sweet Hungarian paprika
> ¹/₄ teaspoon ground cardamom
> ¹/₄ teaspoon ground cinnamon
> ¹/₄ teaspoon turmeric
> ¹/₈ teaspoon cayenne pepper

In a blender, combine all of the ingredients and process until smooth. Use immediately.

Indonesian Curry Marinade

Makes about 1 cup

This is the basic marinade for the chicken saté on page 174, but it is also excellent with pork chops.

$\frac{1}{4}$ cup fresh lime juice
$\frac{1}{4}$ cup soy sauce
$\frac{1}{4}$ cup vegetable oil
2 tablespoons minced shallot or onion
1 tablespoon light brown sugar
2 teaspoons minced fresh ginger
$1\frac{1}{2}$ teaspoons Madras-style curry powder
2 garlic cloves, minced
$\frac{1}{4}$ teaspoon hot red pepper flakes

In a medium glass or nonreactive bowl, whisk together all of the ingredients. Use immediately.

Mustardy Beer Marinade

Makes about 2 cups

Don't choose dark beer or stout—they're too bitter to make a good marinade. Use this on poultry or pork.

> 3 tablespoons spicy brown mustard
> 3 tablespoons light brown sugar
> 3 tablespoons vegetable oil
> 1 tablespoon Worcestershire sauce
> 1 teaspoon hot red pepper sauce, such as Tabasco
> 1 teaspoon salt
> $\frac{1}{2}$ teaspoon freshly ground black pepper
> One 12-ounce can lager beer
> 1 large onion, thinly sliced

In a medium bowl, whisk together the mustard, brown sugar, oil, Worcestershire sauce, hot sauce, salt, and pepper. Stir in the beer and add the onion. Use immediately as a marinade, discarding the onion before grilling the meat or poultry.

Mexican Cerveza and Cilantro Marinade

**FIREFIGHTER RICHARD DUDEN ▪ LADDER COMPANY 167 ▪
NEW YORK FIRE DEPARTMENT ▪ NEW YORK, NEW YORK**

Makes 2⅔ cups

Rick recently transferred from our old firehouse Ladder 129 to Ladder 167 and brought his cooking talents with him. Be sure to add mesquite chips to the fire with this marinade. It's equally good on pork, chicken, or beef.

One 12-ounce can Mexican lager beer
1 medium onion, thinly sliced
½ cup fresh lime juice
⅓ cup olive oil
⅓ cup chopped fresh cilantro
2 tablespoons light brown sugar
1 tablespoon Worcestershire sauce
1 jalapeño pepper, seeded and minced
2 garlic cloves, minced

Combine all of the ingredients in a medium glass or nonreactive bowl. Use immediately or cover tightly with plastic wrap and refrigerate for up to 1 day.

Thai Lemongrass Marinade

Makes about ²/₃ cup

Southeast Asian food is becoming more and more mainstream. While you might have to go to an Asian market for the lemongrass and fish sauce, they just might be at your supermarket, too. Lemongrass is a long stalk with a citrus-like scent and taste that is used as a seasoning. For the marinade you'll only use the tender bottom part of the stalk, but you can add the outer stalks to the coals to give an aromatic smoke (soak the leaves in water for 30 minutes and drain before burning). Fish sauce is a condiment that is used all over Southeast Asia. Just in case you can't find these ingredients, I suggest substitutes.

$\frac{1}{3}$ cup fresh lime juice

$\frac{1}{4}$ cup chopped lemongrass (use the tender bottom part of 3 or 4 stalks), or the grated zest of 1 lime

$\frac{1}{4}$ cup fish sauce or 2 tablespoons Worcestershire sauce, 1 tablespoon soy sauce, and 1 tablespoon water

2 tablespoons vegetable oil

1 tablespoon shredded fresh ginger (use the large holes of a box grater)

1 tablespoon light brown sugar

3 garlic cloves, crushed and peeled

$\frac{1}{2}$ teaspoon hot red pepper flakes

In a blender, process the lime juice, lemongrass, fish sauce, oil, ginger, brown sugar, garlic, and red pepper flakes until the lemon grass and garlic are pureed. Use immediately.

Italian Herb Rub

Makes about 3 tablespoons

This aromatic blend of herbs, garlic, and oil can be rubbed into chicken, pork, swordfish, or beef to add a Mediterranean flavor.

4 garlic cloves
$1\frac{1}{2}$ teaspoons salt
2 tablespoons olive oil
2 teaspoons dried rosemary, crumbled
1 teaspoon dried basil
1 teaspoon dried oregano
1 teaspoon dried sage
$\frac{1}{2}$ teaspoon freshly ground black pepper

Chop the garlic on a work surface. Sprinkle with $\frac{1}{2}$ teaspoon salt. Chop and smear the garlic over the work surface to make a paste. Scrape up and transfer to a small bowl. Stir in the olive oil, rosemary, basil, oregano, sage, the remaining 1 teaspoon salt, and the pepper. Use immediately.

Lone Star Dry Rub

Makes ⅓ cup

Mix up a batch of this dry rub whenever you want to add a kick to your grilled food. It's an indispensable seasoning for smoked beef brisket, but try it on salmon steaks and chicken breasts, too.

>   2 tablespoons chili powder
>   1 tablespoon garlic salt
>   1 tablespoon sweet Hungarian paprika
>   1 tablespoon freshly ground black pepper
>   1 teaspoon cayenne pepper

Mix all of the ingredients together in a bowl or jar. Use immediately or cover and store in a cool, dry place for up to 3 months.

High-Octane Cajun Rub

FIREFIGHTER BOB LA GRANGE (RETIRED) ▪ **VINTON FIRE DEPARTMENT** ▪
VINTON, IOWA

Makes about ³/₄ cup

Bob likes his Cajun seasoning on the hot side. (Afterwards, I've included a variation of my own that is somewhat less hot.) He uses it on tuna steaks, but keep it in mind for beef, chicken, and pork.

> 2 tablespoons garlic powder
> 2 tablespoons dried basil
> 2 tablespoons cayenne pepper
> 2 tablespoons freshly ground black pepper
> 1 tablespoon freshly ground white pepper
> 1 tablespoon onion powder
> 1 tablespoon salt

Mix all of the ingredients in a bowl or jar until combined. Cover and store in a cool, dark place for up to 3 months.

Rookie's Cajun Rub Mix 2 tablespoons sweet Hungarian paprika, 1 tablespoon each dried basil and dried thyme, 1 teaspoon each onion powder and garlic powder, ¹/₂ teaspoon ground black pepper, and ¹/₄ teaspoon cayenne pepper. Makes about ¹/₃ cup.

Italian Green Herb Sauce

Makes about I cup

To Italians, *salsa* means a sauce, not the chunky, spicy condiment of Mexican cuisine, and this is called *salsa verde* ("green sauce"). Serve with grilled fish and poultry.

$^3/_4$ cup packed flat-leaf parsley leaves

$^1/_3$ cup blanched sliced almonds

2 tablespoons chopped fresh basil

2 teaspoons Dijon mustard

2 teaspoons fresh lemon juice

1 teaspoon anchovy paste or 2 anchovy fillets in oil, drained and minced

1 garlic clove, crushed under a knife

$^1/_4$ teaspoon salt

$^1/_4$ teaspoon hot red pepper flakes

$^2/_3$ cup olive oil, preferably extra-virgin

In a blender or food processor, combine the parsley, almonds, basil, mustard, lemon juice, anchovy paste, garlic, salt, and hot pepper flakes. Process to form a paste. With the machine running, gradually add the oil and process until smooth. (The sauce can be prepared up to 1 day ahead, but it is best when served within 2 hours of preparation.)

Lemon-Herb Sauce

Makes about ¹/₂ cup

Here's a simple sauce that can dress up plain grilled fish. It's equally good with mint or oregano, either fresh or dried.

2 tablespoon fresh lemon juice
¹/₄ cup olive oil, preferably extra-virgin
1 tablespoon chopped fresh mint or oregano, or 1 teaspoon dried
¹/₄ teaspoon salt
¹/₄ teaspoon hot red pepper flakes

In a small glass or nonreactive bowl, whisk the lemon juice, olive oil, mint or oregano, salt, and red pepper flakes. Use immediately, or cover and store at room temperature for up to 2 hours.

Classic BBQ Sauce

Makes about 2 cups

What makes this thick, sweet sauce really special is the combination of condiments that go into the pot. All of the ingredients in Worcestershire sauce, steak sauce, mustard, ketchup, and chili sauce combine to give this a flavor that's just right for anything you want to slather it on.

3 tablespoons vegetable oil
1 large onion, finely chopped
2 garlic cloves, minced
1 cup ketchup
1 cup American-style chili sauce
$\frac{1}{2}$ cup packed light brown sugar
$\frac{1}{2}$ cup cider vinegar
2 tablespoons steak sauce, such as A-1
2 tablespoons spicy brown mustard
2 tablespoons Worcestershire sauce

1. In a heavy-bottomed medium saucepan, heat the oil over medium heat. Add the onion and garlic and cook, stirring often, until the onion is golden, about 8 minutes.

2. Stir in the remaining ingredients and bring to a boil. Reduce the heat to low. Simmer, stirring often, until slightly thickened, about 40 minutes. Cool completely. (To store, refrigerate in an airtight container for up to 1 week.)

3. Brush onto food during the last 10 minutes of grilling.

Cup-of-Joe BBQ Sauce

Makes 3 cups

Did you know that coffee is a time-honored ingredient in many barbecue sauces? You'll see how it adds a roasted, toasty flavor that goes perfectly with grilled foods.

2 tablespoons vegetable oil
1 medium onion, chopped
2 garlic cloves, minced
1 cup American-style chili sauce
1 cup strong coffee (I brewed $\frac{1}{4}$ cup ground French roast coffee beans
      and $1\frac{1}{4}$ cups boiling water in a drip pot)
$\frac{1}{2}$ cup ketchup
$\frac{1}{4}$ cup fresh lemon juice
$\frac{1}{4}$ cup unsulphured light molasses
2 tablespoons spicy brown mustard
1 tablespoon Worcestershire sauce
$\frac{1}{2}$ teaspoon hot red pepper flakes

1. In a heavy-bottomed medium saucepan, heat the oil over medium heat. Add the onion and garlic and cook until the onion is golden, about 8 minutes.

2. Stir in the remaining ingredients and bring to a boil. Reduce the heat to low. Simmer, stirring often, until slightly thickened, about 40 minutes. Cool completely. (To store, refrigerate in an airtight container for up to 1 week.)

3. Brush onto food during the last 10 minutes of grilling.

Pepper-Lovers' BBQ Sauce

Makes about 2 cups

Buy a jar of roasted red peppers, and you're on the way to a thick red sauce with zesty Southwestern flavor. This is a fine way to spice up chicken.

One 7-ounce jar roasted red peppers, drained and rinsed
One 4-ounce can mild green chiles, drained and rinsed
1 scallion, white and green parts, chopped
3 tablespoons chopped fresh cilantro
1 garlic clove, minced
2 tablespoons fresh lime juice
2 tablespoons unsulphured light molasses
$1\frac{1}{2}$ teaspoons hot red pepper sauce, such as Tabasco
1 teaspoon ground cumin
1 teaspoon salt
2 tablespoons olive oil

1. In a food processor or blender, process all of the ingredients, except the oil, until smooth.

2. In a large nonstick skillet, heat the oil over medium heat. Add the pepper mixture and bring to a boil. Reduce the heat to low and simmer for 5 minutes, stirring often. Cool completely. (To store, refrigerate in an airtight container for up to 3 days.)

3. Brush onto food during the last 10 minutes of grilling.

Roy's Not-Too-Thick Barbecue Sauce

**FIREFIGHTER ROY DAVIS ▪ TACOMA FIRE DEPARTMENT ▪
FOX ISLAND, WASHINGTON**

Makes 1½ cups

Roy is a retired Air Force pilot who is now enjoying a second career as a fire-fighter. Roy holds the world record in the over-50 category in the Firefight-ers Combat Challenge, which is a grueling obstacle-course competition replicating all the major firefighting tasks. In addition, he and his wife own a quaint bed-and-breakfast, where guests sometimes sample Roy's cooking skills. His barbecue sauce is on the thin side—it's for people who don't like sweet sauces.

> ½ cup soy sauce, preferably a Japanese brand
> ½ cup ketchup
> ¼ cup dry white wine
> 3 tablespoons dried minced onions
> 3 tablespoons yellow mustard
> 2 tablespoons sugar
> 2 tablespoons unsalted butter
> ¼ teaspoon garlic powder
> ¼ teaspoon chili powder
> ¼ teaspoon freshly ground black pepper

1. Bring all of the ingredients to a boil in a medium saucepan over medium heat, stirring often. Reduce the heat to medium-low and simmer for 5 minutes, until slightly thickened. Cool completely. (To store, refrigerate in an airtight container for up to 3 days.)

2. Brush onto food during the last 10 minutes of grilling.

Fire-Eater's Sauce

FIREFIGHTER GREG WEBER ▪ LINDEN FIRE DEPARTMENT ▪ LINDEN, NEW JERSEY

Makes about 4 cups

One thing I've noticed about BBQ sauce recipes: the more stuff in them, the better they are. To brew his version, Greg uses not one, but three different hot pepper sauces—each with its own distinct flavor. While this thin sauce can be used for basting grilled meats and poultry, Greg also likes to serve it as a dipping sauce. It makes a big batch, but keeps for a long time in a covered container in the refrigerator.

1 cup ketchup
1 cup store-bought barbecue sauce
$\frac{1}{2}$ cup soy sauce
$\frac{1}{2}$ cup packed light brown sugar
6 garlic cloves, minced
$\frac{1}{4}$ cup honey
3 tablespoons store-bought thick teriyaki glaze
2 tablespoons Worcestershire sauce
2 teaspoons freshly ground black pepper
1 tablespoon garlic powder
1 tablespoon onion powder
1 teaspoon hot green jalapeño-flavored sauce, such as Tabasco
1 teaspoon hot red pepper sauce, such as Tabasco
1 teaspoon Louisiana-style hot sauce, such as Frank's

1. In a large heavy-bottomed saucepan, combine all of the ingredients with $\frac{1}{2}$ cup water. Bring to a simmer over medium heat, stirring often. Reduce the heat to low and simmer until slightly thickened, about 10 minutes. Cool completely. (To store, refrigerate in a covered container for up to 2 weeks.)

2. Brush onto food during the last 10 minutes of grilling.

Argentine Steak Sauce

Makes about 1½ cups

Any Argentine steak house worth its salt has to have a bottle of vinegary green *chimichurri* on the table. Think of it as their version of A-1 Steak Sauce.

> 1 cup fresh parsley leaves
> ³/₄ cup extra-virgin or regular olive oil
> ¹/₄ cup minced onion
> ¹/₄ cup red wine vinegar
> 4 garlic cloves, crushed under a knife
> 1 teaspoon dried oregano
> ¹/₂ teaspoon salt
> ¹/₂ teaspoon freshly ground black pepper

In a blender or food processor fitted with a metal blade, combine all of the ingredients and process just until mixed, about 10 seconds. (The sauce can be prepared up to 5 days ahead, covered, and stored in the refrigerator, but it is best if used within a few hours of making.) Serve as a sauce with grilled beef.

Mango Chutney Glaze

Makes about 1¹/₂ cups

You'll have a hard time deciding if this is better on chicken or pork. Mango chutney is sometimes labeled "Major Grey's" chutney.

One 8¹/₂-ounce jar mango chutney
¹/₃ cup rice vinegar
1 tablespoon spicy brown mustard
1 tablespoon light brown sugar
1 teaspoon Madras-style curry powder (optional)
¹/₄ teaspoon cayenne pepper

In a blender or food processor fitted with a metal blade, puree all of the ingredients. Use as a glaze, brushing onto food during the last 5 to 10 minutes of grilling.

Plum-Ginger Glaze

Makes 1 1/2 cups

Ripe, juicy eating plums, such as the Santa Rosa variety, are best for making this Asian-style glaze. (Save the purple Italian prune plums for desserts.) Brush this onto pork chops, spareribs, or chicken.

1 pound ripe plums, such as Santa Rosa, pitted and coarsely chopped
2 tablespoons shredded fresh ginger (use the large holes of a box grater)
2 tablespoons rice vinegar
2 tablespoons light brown sugar
1 tablespoon Dijon mustard
1 garlic clove, pressed
1/4 teaspoon hot red pepper flakes

1. In a medium saucepan, combine all of the ingredients and bring to a simmer over medium heat, stirring occasionally. Reduce the heat to low and cover. Simmer until the plums are very tender, about 10 minutes.

2. Transfer to a blender and process until smooth. Cool completely. Cover and refrigerate until ready to use, up to 3 days.

3. Use as a glaze, brushing onto food during the last 5 to 10 minutes of grilling.

Honey-Mustard Glaze

Makes about I cup

Great on chicken. Try this on shrimp, too.

$^2/_3$ cup Dijon mustard
$^1/_4$ cup honey
2 tablespoons finely chopped scallions, white parts only
2 teaspoons soy sauce
$^1/_2$ teaspoon hot red pepper flakes

1. In a small bowl, mix all of the ingredients. Cover and refrigerate until ready to use, up to 2 days.

2. Use as a glaze, brushing onto food during the last 5 to 10 minutes of grilling.

Fish and Shellfish

Classic Grilled Fish Steaks

Makes 6 servings

With some people, a backyard grillout always features red meat. But, I live on Long Island, and that is fish country. The sizzle coming from my backyard grill is just as likely to be caused by a grilled salmon steak as a T-bone.

I prefer grilling tuna, swordfish, and salmon steaks to fish fillets, because so many fish fillets break apart when you turn them. (I solve the problem by cooking delicate fillets in a foil pouch with vegetables—see Red Snapper with Creole Vegetables in Foil Pouches on page 92.) Don't overcook fish steaks, or they may dry out. Most people prefer tuna and swordfish cooked to medium-rare—use the sharp tip of a knife to check the center of the fish, which should look barely opaque.

Regardless of the type of fish you are grilling, never marinate it for too long—30 minutes is usually enough time, and 1 hour is tops. Acids in the marinade (such as wine, citrus juice, or vinegar) will "cook" the delicate flesh and toughen it. Maybe you've had seviche in a Mexican restaurant, which is fish marinated in lime juice until it turns firm. Believe me, grilled seviche isn't that great. While marinating, if you notice that the edges of the fish are turning bright white, that means the acid is doing what comes naturally. Immediately remove the fish from the marinade, and cook it as soon as possible.

Grilled fish has a tendency to stick to the cooking grate. To avoid this problem, be sure your grate is well-cleaned—give it a real scrub with the grill brush—and oil it well. Brush the fish lightly with oil, too. Don't bother oiling marinated fish, as most marinades will already include oil.

Simply grilled fish goes with a number of condiments. Italian Green Herb Sauce is a good choice, but try Summer Vegetable Salsa (page 29) and Mango-Jalapeño Salsa (page 30) some other time.

Four 6- to 8-ounce swordfish, tuna, or salmon steaks, cut $^3/_4$ inch thick
1 tablespoon olive oil
$^1/_4$ teaspoon salt
$^1/_4$ teaspoon freshly ground black pepper
Italian Green Herb Sauce (page 72)

1. Build a charcoal fire in an outdoor grill and let burn until the coals are covered with white ashes. **IN A GAS GRILL,** preheat on High.

2. Lightly oil the cooking grate. Brush the fish steaks with the oil and season with the salt and pepper. Place on the grill and cover. Grill, turning once, just until the fish is opaque when pierced in the center with the tip of a sharp knife, about 6 minutes. Serve immediately, with the sauce passed on the side.

Monkfish with Red Pepper-Basil Sauce

Makes 4 servings

If you've ever seen a whole monkfish, you probably thought you'd never seen an uglier fish. But its sweet-tasting meat is delicious, and we cook it at the firehouse often. The long, meaty fillets are cut from the tail and look like shelled lobster tail; they taste somewhat like lobster, too.

RED PEPPER-BASIL SAUCE

3 medium red bell peppers, roasted, peeled, seeded, and coarsely
    chopped (page 27)
1 tablespoon fresh lemon juice
2 garlic cloves, crushed through a press
3 tablespoons extra-virgin olive oil
$\frac{1}{4}$ teaspoon salt
2 tablespoons finely chopped fresh basil

Four 7-ounce monkfish fillets
White Wine and Herb Marinade (page 58)

1. To make the sauce, purée the peppers, lemon juice, and garlic in a food processor. With the machine running, add the oil. Season with the salt. Pour into a bowl and let stand at room temperature until ready to serve, up to 2 hours, or refrigerate for up to 1 day. (Remove chilled sauce from refrigerator 1 hour before serving.)

2. Combine the fish and marinade in a zippered plastic bag. Seal the bag and let stand at room temperature for 30 minutes, no longer.

3. Build a charcoal fire (use about $2\frac{1}{2}$ pounds of briquettes) on one side of an outdoor grill and let it burn until the coals are covered with white ash. **IN A GAS GRILL,** preheat on High, then turn one burner off and adjust the other burner(s) to High.

4. Lightly oil the cooking grate. Drain the fish well, but do not scrape off the clinging herbs. Place the fish over the coals and cover. Grill, turning occasionally, until browned on all sides, about 6 minutes. **IN A GAS GRILL,** place the fish over the High burner and cover. Grill, turning occasionally, until browned on all sides, about 6 minutes.

5. Transfer the fish to the cooler side of the grill (or over the off burner). Cook until the fish is opaque when flaked in the center, about 6 more minutes.

6. Cut each fillet crosswise into thick slices. Transfer the slices to dinner plates. Stir the basil into the sauce. Serve the fish immediately, with the sauce passed on the side.

Wine-Smoked Salmon Fillets

**LT. WILFRED "WOLF" SCHMELZINGER (RETIRED) ▪ ENGINE COMPANY 319 ▪
NEW YORK FIRE DEPARTMENT ▪ NEW YORK, NEW YORK**

Makes 4 servings

Lt. "Wolf" Schmelzinger is enjoying retired life and is adding to the reputation he had as an excellent cook when he was in the department. He was the inspiration for the patch representing Engine 319, a single engine company: "The Lone Wolf."

> 2 cups oak, alder, or hickory wood chips
> 3 cups inexpensive, but tasty, dry white wine
> $\frac{1}{4}$ cup grainy "country style" French mustard
> 1 tablespoon light brown sugar
> 1 tablespoon chopped fresh dill
> Four 7-ounce salmon fillets, with skin
> 2 teaspoons vegetable oil

1. In a medium bowl, soak the hickory chips in the wine for at least 30 minutes. Drain the chips, reserving the wine. Set the chips and wine aside.

2. Meanwhile, using about $2\frac{1}{2}$ pounds of briquettes, build a charcoal fire on one side of an outdoor grill. Let the fire burn until medium-hot—you should be able to hold your hand at grate level to a count of three—and the coals are covered with white ash. Place an empty aluminum foil pan on the empty side of the grill. Pour the wine into the pan. Sprinkle a handful of chips over the coals and cover. **IN A GAS GRILL,** preheat on High. Turn one burner off and the other burner(s) to Medium. Place an empty aluminum foil pan over the "Off" burner. Pour the wine into the pan. Place the drained chips in a metal chip box. Or, wrap the drained chips in aluminum foil, pierce a few holes in the foil, and place the foil packet on the heat source. Cover and allow a few minutes for the chips to build up a head of smoke.

3. In a small bowl, mix the mustard, brown sugar, and dill, dissolving the sugar. Brush the salmon skin with the oil. Spread the mustard mixture on the flesh side of the salmon.

4. Lightly oil the cooking grate. Place the fish fillets, skin-side down, over the pan. Cover and smoke until the salmon looks opaque when prodded in the center with the tip of a knife, 20 to 25 minutes.

5. Using a wide spatula, transfer the fillets to dinner plates. If the salmon skin sticks to the grate, slide the spatula between the skin and flesh, and lift off the salmon, leaving the skin on the grill. Serve immediately.

Mesquite Salmon Steaks with Summer Vegetable Salsa

Makes 4 servings

Smoked with mesquite, seasoned with chili powder, and served with salsa, these steaks have a Tex-Mex kick. Because the salmon won't be smoked for long, be sure the mesquite builds up a good head of smoke before placing the fish on the grill so it can start smoking from the get-go.

> Four 7-ounce salmon steaks
> 1 tablespoon olive oil
> 1 tablespoon chili powder
> $\frac{1}{2}$ teaspoon salt
> 1 cup mesquite wood chips, soaked in water for 30 minutes and drained
> Summer Vegetable Salsa (page 29)

1. Build a charcoal fire in an outdoor grill and let burn until the coals are covered with white ash. Sprinkle the drained chips over the coals. **IN A GAS GRILL,** preheat on High. Place the drained chips in the metal smoke box. Or, wrap the drained chips in aluminum foil, pierce a few holes in the foil, and place on the heat source. Cover and let the chips smolder until a good stream of smoke can be seen coming from the lid.

2. Lightly oil the cooking grate. Brush the salmon on both sides with the oil. Season with the chili powder and salt. Place the salmon on the grill and cover. Grill, without turning, until the salmon flakes with a fork, about 7 minutes. Serve immediately, garnishing each serving with a spoonful of salsa.

Grilled Snapper Fillets with Vera Cruz Sauce

Makes 4 servings

If you are going to grill fish fillets, invest in a wire grilling basket to make turning easier. This recipe features a spicy tomato-and-pickled-jalapeño sauce. (Pickled jalapeños aren't hard to find these days, thanks to the popularity of nachos.) Grilling the tomatoes first makes this sauce distinctive. Serve this with plenty of warmed tortillas.

2 tablespoons olive oil
1 tablespoon fresh lime juice
$^1/_4$ teaspoon salt
Four 7-ounce snapper fillets

VERA CRUZ SAUCE

$1^1/_2$ pounds ripe plum tomatoes
2 tablespoons olive oil
1 medium onion, chopped
2 garlic cloves, minced
1 pickled jalapeño pepper, seeded and minced, plus 1 tablespoon juice
    from the jar
1 teaspoon dried oregano
$^1/_4$ teaspoon salt
$^1/_3$ cup sliced pimiento-stuffed olives

1. In a small bowl, whisk together the oil, lime juice, and salt. Place in a zippered plastic bag and add the fish. Close the bag and refrigerate for 30 minutes, no longer.

2. Build a charcoal fire in an outdoor grill and let the fire burn until covered with white ash. **IN A GAS GRILL,** preheat on High.

3. Lightly oil a cooking grate. Grill the tomatoes, turning occasionally, until the skins are charred on all sides, about 6 minutes. Let cool until easy to handle. Peel the tomatoes. In a food processor, coarsely chop the tomatoes.

continued

4. In a medium saucepan, heat the oil over medium heat. Add the onion and garlic and cook, stirring often, until the onion softens, about 5 minutes. Stir in the tomatoes, jalapeño and juice, oregano, and salt. Bring to a simmer and reduce the heat to low. Simmer until the tomato juices thicken, about 15 minutes. Stir in the olives and cook until heated through, about 5 minutes. Keep the sauce warm on the side of the grill.

5. Add more briquettes to the fire and let burn until covered with white ash and medium-hot. You should be able to hold your hand over the coals at grate level for 3 seconds. **IN A GAS GRILL,** adjust the heat to Medium. Lightly oil both sides of a wire fish grilling basket. Place the fillets in the basket.

6. Grill uncovered, turning once, until the fish flakes with a fork, about 6 minutes. Serve immediately, with the sauce.

Red Snapper with Creole Vegetables in Foil Pouches

Makes 4 servings

Grilling fish in a foil pouch is a good way to cook delicate fish fillets outdoors. You won't have to worry about the fish breaking when you turn it. Serve with hot cooked rice to soak up all the spicy juices.

> 1 large yellow summer squash, cut into 2-inch by $^{1}/_{4}$-inch strips
> 1 large red bell pepper, cut into 2-inch by $^{1}/_{4}$-inch strips
> 2 medium shallots, thinly sliced and separated into rounds ($^{1}/_{3}$ cup)
> 1 tablespoon Rookie's Cajun Rub (page 71)
> $^{1}/_{2}$ teaspoon salt
> Nonstick vegetable oil spray
> Four 4- to 5-ounce red snapper fillets
> 6 plum tomatoes, cut into $^{1}/_{2}$-inch rounds
> 6 tablespoons fresh lime juice
> 6 tablespoons olive oil

1. Build a charcoal fire in an outdoor grill and let burn until the coals are covered with white ash. Let burn down until medium-hot—you should be able to hold your hand at grate level for 3 seconds. **IN A GAS GRILL,** preheat on High, then adjust to Medium.

2. In a medium bowl, mix the squash, red pepper, and shallots. In a small bowl, mix the Cajun rub and salt. Set the two bowls aside.

3. Tear off six 20-inch lengths of aluminum foil. Fold one piece of foil in half vertically; unfold. Spray the foil with nonstick spray. On one side of the fold, place one-sixth of the vegetable mixture. Top with a snapper fillet. Season the vegetables and fish with the seasoning mixture. Arrange one tomato, overlapping the slices, on top of the fillet. Drizzle with 1 tablespoon *each* of the lime juice and oil. Fold the foil over to cover the fish and vegetables, then tightly fold the three open sides of the foil to seal. Fold over the fourth side of the foil to form a rectangle with four folded sides. Repeat with the remaining foil and ingredients.

4. Place the foil pouches on the grill and cover. Grill, without turning, until the fish is opaque when flaked in the center with the tip of a knife (open a pouch to check), about 10 minutes. Open each pouch, and transfer the vegetables and fish to each plate with a wide spatula, pouring the juices over the top. Or, allow the diners to cut open their pouches at the table, using sharp steak knives.

Swordfish and Bay Leaf Kebabs

Makes 4 servings

No, you don't eat the bay leaves, but as they grill (and singe), they give off an aromatic smoke that flavors the swordfish. This is especially tasty served with the Grilled Red Peppers with Balsamic Vinegar and Garlic (page 50) or Bruce's Grilled Parmesan Zucchini (page 47).

2 tablespoons olive oil
$\frac{1}{4}$ teaspoon salt
$\frac{1}{4}$ teaspoon hot red pepper flakes
$1\frac{3}{4}$ pounds swordfish steaks, skin removed, cut into twenty ($1\frac{1}{2}$-inch) cubes
24 dried imported bay leaves
Lemon-Herb Sauce (page 73), (made with oregano)

1. Soak four 12-inch bamboo skewers in water for 30 minutes. Then drain. Build a charcoal fire in an outdoor grill and let burn until the coals are covered with white ashes. **IN A GAS GRILL,** preheat on High.

2. In a medium bowl, whisk together the oil, salt, and red pepper flakes. Add the swordfish cubes and bay leaves and toss to coat. Thread 5 swordfish cubes and 6 bay leaves onto each skewer, beginning and ending with a bay leaf.

3. Lightly oil the cooking grate. Place the kebabs on the grill and cover. Grill, turning once, until the swordfish is just opaque in the center when prodded with the tip of a sharp knife, 6 to 7 minutes. Serve, drizzling each serving with a spoonful of the dressing.

Swordfish with Grilled Fennel

**FIREFIGHTER MICHAEL BONANNO (RETIRED) ▪ LADDER COMPANY 7 ▪
NEW YORK FIRE DEPARTMENT ▪ NEW YORK, NEW YORK**

Makes 4 servings

Not enough cooks know about fennel, unless they're Italian, and then it shows up on the table a lot, especially in the fall. Fennel grills up beautifully, goes well with grilled fish like this swordfish. This is from my brother, Michael, who was also a fireman. He received an injury that ended his firefighting career, but now he lives in Morro Bay, California, where he cooks plenty of local fish and produce.

> Four 6-ounce swordfish steaks, skin removed
> White Wine and Herb Marinade (page 58)
> 2 medium fennel bulbs
> Lemon wedges

1. Build a charcoal fire in an outdoor grill and let burn until the coals are covered with white ash. **IN A GAS GRILL,** preheat on High.

2. Combine the swordfish and marinade in a zippered plastic bag. Close the bag and let stand at room temperature for 30 minutes, no longer.

3. Cut off and discard any feathery tops from the fennel bulbs, and remove the tough outer layer. Cut each bulb vertically into ¼-inch-thick slices. Just before grilling, add the fennel to the plastic bag and coat well with the marinade.

4. Lightly oil the cooking grate. Place the fennel on the grill and cover. Grill for 2 minutes, turn once, and grill for an additional 2 minutes. Add the swordfish and cover. Grill, turning the fish once, just until the fish is opaque when pierced in the center with the tip of a sharp knife and the fennel is tender, about 6 minutes.

Stuffed Sicilian Swordfish

Makes 6 servings

Stuffed with the familiar Sicilian trio of roasted red pepper, anchovies, and garlic, these swordfish steaks are out of the ordinary. They are served with a simple dressing of lemon juice, olive oil, and fresh herbs—a good, easy sauce to keep in mind for other grilled fish. Be sure your knife is good and sharp before you slice open the swordfish steaks.

> Six 6-ounce swordfish steaks, skin removed
> 1 small red bell pepper, roasted (page 27), seeded, and cut into 6 pieces
> 6 anchovy fillets soaked in oil, drained
> 6 large fresh basil leaves
> 2 garlic cloves, minced
> 1 tablespoon olive oil
> Salt, to taste
> Freshly ground black pepper, to taste
> Lemon-Herb Sauce (page 73)

1. Using a sharp, thin-bladed knife, butterfly each swordfish steak by cutting horizontally through the center, reaching almost to, but not through, the opposite side, so each steak can be opened like a book. On one side of each steak, place a piece of red pepper (trimmed to fit, if necessary), an anchovy fillet, a basil leaf, and a sprinkle of fresh garlic. Fold the steak over to enclose the filling, and secure with wooden toothpicks. Brush each steak with oil and season with salt and pepper. Cover and let stand at room temperature while building the fire.

2. Build a charcoal fire in an outdoor grill and let burn until the coals are covered with white ash. **IN A GAS GRILL,** preheat on High.

3. Lightly oil the cooking grate. Place the swordfish on the grill and cover. Grill the swordfish, turning once, just until the fish is opaque when prodded with the tip of a knife, 6 to 7 minutes. Do not overcook.

4. Serve the swordfish, drizzling each portion with a spoonful of the sauce.

Marinated Tuna and Mushroom Kebabs

Makes 4 servings

Tuna stands up to hearty marinades and goes well with mushrooms, too. I usually use medium-sized supermarket-variety white button mushrooms, but if you want to go gourmet, substitute a large portobello cap, cut into eight wedges. Don't soak the mushrooms in the marinade—a quick dip will do the trick—or they will soak it up like a sponge.

$1\frac{1}{2}$ pounds tuna, skin removed, cut into sixteen ($1\frac{1}{2}$-inch) chunks
Tuscan Red Wine Marinade (page 59)
8 medium white (button) mushroom caps
12 cherry tomatoes

1. Soak four 12-inch bamboo skewers in water for 30 minutes. Then drain. Combine the fish and marinade in a zippered plastic bag. Close the bag and let stand at room temperature for 30 minutes to 1 hour, no longer. Just before making the kebabs, toss the mushrooms and cherry tomatoes in the marinade.

2. Remove the fish, mushrooms, and tomatoes from the marinade, reserving the marinade. For each kebab, alternate 4 tuna cubes, 2 mushrooms, and 3 cherry tomatoes on each skewer, beginning and ending with a tomato.

3. Meanwhile, build a charcoal fire in an outdoor grill and let burn until the coals are covered with white ash. **IN A GAS GRILL,** preheat on High.

4. Lightly oil the cooking grate. Place the kebabs on the grill and cover. Grill, turning occasionally, until the tuna chunks are rosy-red when pierced in the center, about 6 minutes for medium-rare tuna. Serve immediately.

Grilled Tuna Salad with Potatoes and Green Beans

Makes 6 servings

Tuna salad, made with canned tuna, is a popular lunch item around the firehouse. I couldn't help imagining how terrific it would be with *grilled* tuna.

LEMON-ROSEMARY DRESSING

$^1/_2$ cup fresh lemon juice
$^1/_2$ teaspoon salt
$^1/_2$ teaspoon hot red pepper flakes
$1^1/_2$ cups olive oil
1 tablespoon chopped fresh rosemary or 1 teaspoon dried

$1^1/_2$ pounds tuna steak, cut $^3/_4$ inch thick, skin removed
6 ounces green beans, trimmed
1 pound medium new potatoes, scrubbed but unpeeled, cut into $^3/_4$-inch-wide wedges
8 cups mesclun or mixed salad greens
2 ripe medium tomatoes, cut into sixths
2 hard-cooked eggs, cut into slices

1. To make the lemon dressing, whisk together the lemon juice, salt, and red pepper in a small bowl. Gradually whisk in the oil. Stir in the rosemary. In a zippered plastic bag, pour $^1/_2$ cup of the lemon dressing over the tuna. Close the bag and let stand at room temperature for 30 minutes, no longer. Set the remaining dressing aside.

2. Build a charcoal fire in an outdoor grill and let burn until the coals are covered with white ash. **IN A GAS GRILL,** preheat on High.

3. Meanwhile, bring a medium saucepan of lightly salted water to a boil over high heat. Add the green beans and cook until barely tender, about 3 minutes. Using a large skimmer or slotted spoon, remove the green beans to a colander, and rinse under cold running water until cool. Set aside.

4. Add the potatoes to the saucepan of boiling water. Cook until the potatoes are almost, but not quite, tender, about 7 minutes. Drain and rinse under cold water. Just before grilling, toss the potatoes with the tuna and dressing.

5. Lightly oil the cooking grate. Grill the potatoes, covered, turning occasionally, until golden brown, about 5 minutes. Move to the cooler outer perimeter of the grate, not directly over the coals, to keep warm. **IN A GAS GRILL,** transfer the potatoes to a flameproof bowl and cover with foil. Just before serving, return to the grill and cook for 1 or 2 minutes to reheat.

6. Grill the tuna, covered, turning once, until the center looks rosy-red when pierced in the center, about 6 minutes. Transfer the tuna to a cutting board, and cut crosswise into ½-inch-thick strips.

7. Place the mesclun on a large, deep platter. Drizzle with half of the reserved dressing and toss. Arrange the tuna over the mesclun, then scatter the potatoes, tomatoes, green beans, and hard-cooked eggs around the tuna. Drizzle with the remaining reserved dressing. Serve immediately.

Bob's Grilled Cajun Tuna Steaks

**FIREFIGHTER BOB LA GRANGE (RETIRED) ▪ VINTON FIRE DEPARTMENT ▪
VINTON, IOWA**

Makes 4 servings

Now that Bob is retired, he has more time to grill his favorite dishes, like these spice-dipped tuna steaks. In his recipe, Bob repeated one of the premier rules of tuna-grilling in capital letters: "DO NOT OVERCOOK." These are good served with Summer Vegetable Salsa (page 29).

Four 6- to 8-ounce tuna steaks, skin removed, cut $^3/_4$ inch thick
2 tablespoons canola oil
2 tablespoons High-Octane Cajun Rub or Rookie's Cajun Rub (page 71)

1. Build a charcoal fire in an outdoor grill and let burn until the coals are covered with white ash. **IN A GAS GRILL,** preheat on High.

2. Meanwhile, brush both sides of the fish steaks with the oil. Sprinkle with the rub. Let stand at room temperature while waiting for the fire to reach proper temperature.

3. Lightly oil the cooking grate. Grill the tuna, covered, turning once, until the steaks are rosy-red when pierced in the center, about 6 minutes for medium-rare tuna. Serve immediately.

Mediterranean Grilled Tuna Fish Sandwich

Makes 4 servings

Instead of mayonnaise-based tuna salad sandwiches, try this special grilled tuna version, served on a French roll with a garlicky vinaigrette dressing. The dressing acts as a marinade, too.

> $^{1}/_{4}$ cup red wine vinegar
> 2 garlic cloves, crushed through a press
> $^{1}/_{2}$ teaspoon salt
> $^{1}/_{2}$ teaspoon hot red pepper flakes
> 1 cup olive oil
> Four 6-ounce tuna steaks, cut about $^{1}/_{2}$ inch thick
> 4 crusty French or Italian rolls, split
> 2 medium tomatoes, thinly sliced
> 1 small red onion, thinly sliced
> 1 bunch arugula, well-rinsed and dried
> 2 hard-cooked eggs, thinly sliced (optional)

1. In a small bowl, whisk together the vinegar, garlic, salt, and hot pepper. Gradually whisk in the oil. Pour $^{1}/_{2}$ cup dressing into a zippered plastic bag, and set the remaining dressing aside. Add the tuna and close the bag. Let stand at room temperature for 30 minutes, no longer.

2. Build a charcoal fire in an outdoor grill and let burn until the coals are covered with white ash. **IN A GAS GRILL,** preheat on High.

3. Remove the tuna from the bag and reserve the dressing. Lightly oil the cooking grate. Place the tuna on the grill and cover. Grill, turning once, just until the tuna is rosy-red when pierced in the center, about 6 minutes.

4. Pull out a bit of the inner crumb from each roll—this way, you'll be able to taste more filling than bread. Drizzle the insides of each roll with about 2 tablespoons dressing. Make each roll into a sandwich with a tuna steak topped with tomato, onion slices, arugula, and the egg slices, if using. Serve immediately.

Grilled Clams with Parsley-Garlic Butter

**FIREFIGHTER MIKE KEELY • ENGINE COMPANY 299 •
NEW YORK FIRE DEPARTMENT • NEW YORK, NEW YORK**

Makes 4 servings

Mike has one of the longest commutes to work in Queens, but loves living out on Long Island, where he has access to great seafood. Clams are especially abundant on the "East End" of the island, and cooks are always looking for ways to make them. This grilled version is one of the best, and be sure to serve it with lots of crusty bread for dipping. (If you wish, substitute olive oil for the butter, or mussels for the clams.)

Mollusks, such as mussels, clams, and oysters, should be purchased only from reliable sources. On Long Island and at other seaside areas, they are often sold from roadside stands, but be sure the purveyors display an inspection certificate, as they could be collecting their merchandise illegally from polluted waters.

Before grilling, soak mollusks in a large bowl or sink of cold water with $\frac{1}{4}$ cup cornmeal for 30 minutes. This helps them expel any grit or sand.

> 8 tablespoons (1 stick) unsalted butter
> 3 garlic cloves, minced
> 3 tablespoons fresh lemon juice
> 2 tablespoons chopped fresh parsley
> $\frac{1}{8}$ teaspoon freshly ground black pepper
> 4 dozen cherrystone clams, scrubbed, soaked, and drained

1. Build a charcoal fire in an outdoor grill and let burn until the coals are covered with white ash. **IN A GAS GRILL,** preheat on High.

2. In a small saucepan, melt the butter with the garlic over medium-low heat. Then simmer for 1 minute. Remove from the heat and stir in the lemon juice, parsley, and pepper. Keep the butter warm.

3. Place the clams on the grill and cover. Grill until the clams open, about 5 minutes. As the clams open, transfer with tongs to a 15- by 10-inch aluminum foil baking pan. If some of the clams remain stubbornly shut, rap them a couple of times with the tongs, and they should open. Discard any unopened clams. Let the clams cool slightly, then remove the top half of the shell (without the clam meat). Spoon a dab of garlic butter in each clam shell, reserving any remaining garlic butter.

4. Place the aluminum pan with the clams on the grill. Cover with the grill lid and cook until the clam juices are bubbling, about 5 minutes. Serve the clams directly from the pan, with small bowls of extra garlic butter for dipping.

Grilled Mussels with Garlic Butter Substitute 4 dozen mussels, beards removed, for the clams. (Farm-raised mussels will not have beards.)

Grilled Lobster Halves
with Lemon-Herb Butter

FIREFIGHTER JOHN TREZZA ▪ ENGINE COMPANY 273 ▪
NEW YORK FIRE DEPARTMENT ▪ NEW YORK, NEW YORK

Makes 2 servings

John was chosen from many entrants to be a "calendar boy" on the New York Firefighters Hunk Calendar. Even though John had to endure more than his share of ribbing over the photo, he actually got quite a few other modeling jobs, and money from the calendar went to the New York Firefighters Burn Center. John's recipe serves only two—it's hard to fit more than two lobster on a grill—and is perfect for romantic dinners. Grilled lobster can dry out a little, so keep it well-basted with the aromatic butter.

> 4 tablespoons ($^1/_2$ stick) unsalted butter
> 2 tablespoons fresh lemon juice
> Grated zest of 1 lemon
> 2 teaspoons chopped fresh tarragon or 1 teaspoon dried
> 2 teaspoons chopped fresh chives
> Two $1^1/_4$- to $1^1/_2$-pound live lobsters
> $^1/_4$ teaspoon salt
> $^1/_4$ teaspoon freshly ground black pepper
> $^3/_4$ cup fresh breadcrumbs, made from slightly stale Italian bread

1. Build a charcoal fire in an outdoor grill and let burn until the coals are covered with white ash. **IN A GAS GRILL,** preheat on High.

2. In a small saucepan, combine the butter, lemon juice and zest, tarragon, and chives. Melt the butter over low heat. Set the butter aside.

3. Using a heavy knife, cut the lobsters at the crease behind the head—do not cut them completely through. Split the lobsters in half lengthwise. Remove the dark matter in the heads, and discard the intestinal tube that runs the length of each one. Reserve any green tomalley or red roe you might find and stir these into the melted butter. Crack the lobster claws. Brush all of the cut surfaces of the lobsters with some of the melted herb butter. Season with the salt and pepper.

4. Oil the cooking grate well. Place the lobsters, cut sides down, on the grill and cover. Grill the lobsters until the lobster meat is opaque on the surface, about 3 minutes. Turn the lobsters and brush with the herb butter. Sprinkle the lobster halves with the breadcrumbs and drizzle with the remaining butter. Cover and grill until the shells are deep red, the crust is golden, and the lobster meat is opaque in the center when prodded with the tip of a knife, 10 to 15 minutes. Serve immediately.

Barbecued Oysters

Makes 6 appetizer servings

In northern California, juicy oysters hot off the grill rival chilled oysters on the half shell. They're really a hit at firehouse community barbecues around Tomales Bay, where there are extensive oyster beds. Use your favorite tomato-based barbecue sauce, but I am partial to my own Cup-of-Joe BBQ Sauce. It's hard to say how many of these constitutes a serving—I'm estimating four each as an appetizer. If you have a bunch of firefighters around, they could eat a dozen each and still have room for dinner.

$\frac{1}{2}$ cup Cup-of-Joe BBQ Sauce (page 75)
2 dozen large oysters, on the half-shell (see Note)
Lemon wedges

1. Build a charcoal fire in an outdoor grill and let burn until the coals are covered with white ash. **IN A GAS GRILL,** preheat on High.

2. Spoon a heaping teaspoon of sauce into each oyster shell. Place the oysters on the grill and cover. Cook just until the sauce is bubbling, about 3 minutes. Using tongs, transfer the oysters to serving plates, being careful not to spill the juices in the shells. Serve immediately, with the lemon wedges.

Note Ask your fish purveyor to open the oysters for you. If you have to open the oysters at home, there is a much easier way than with an oyster knife. It calls for an old-fashioned, pointed can opener. Place a rinsed and well-scrubbed oyster, curved side down, on a folded kitchen towel. Oysters are usually teardrop-shaped. Locate the spot where the top shell meets the bottom shell at the pointed tip of the "teardrop." Pointed end up, wedge the point of the can opener into the crack about $\frac{1}{4}$ inch below the tip of the shell. Push the end of the can opener downward, and the shell should pop open from the leverage. Run a small sharp knife around the top shell to release it. Slip the knife under the flat top shell to cut the oyster free, and discard the top shell. Run the knife underneath the oyster in the curved bottom shell to loosen the oyster meat. Refrigerate the opened oysters until ready to grill.

Grilled Scallop Kebabs with Italian Crumb Crust

FIREFIGHTER PAUL LAMPASSO ▪ ENGINE COMPANY 299 ▪ NEW YORK FIRE DEPARTMENT ▪ NEW YORK, NEW YORK

Makes 4 servings

Paul is an avid cook, and a big fan of all the television cooking shows. He is also a pilot who is building his own plane. Here's his easy recipe for grilled scallop kebabs. Crumb-coating the scallops helps to keep them moist. These kebabs don't have any vegetables, so be sure to serve them with a hearty side dish like Gazpacho Salad (page 35).

> 2 tablespoons olive oil
> 1 garlic clove, crushed through a press
> $\frac{1}{4}$ teaspoon hot red pepper flakes
> 16 large sea scallops (about $1\frac{1}{4}$ pounds)
> $\frac{1}{2}$ cup dried breadcrumbs
> 1 teaspoon dried oregano
> Lemon wedges

1. Soak four 12-inch bamboo skewers in water for 30 minutes. Then drain. Build a charcoal fire in an outdoor grill and let burn until the coals are covered with white ash. **IN A GAS GRILL** preheat on High.

2. In a small bowl, mix the oil, garlic, and hot red peppers. Add the scallops and toss to coat. On a shallow plate, mix the breadcrumbs and oregano. Roll the scallops in the breadcrumbs and thread onto the skewers. Do not let the scallops touch each other.

3. Lightly oil the cooking grate. Grill, turning occasionally, until the crumb coating is golden brown on all sides, about 5 minutes. Serve immediately, with the lemon wedges.

Grilled Shrimp on Pasta with Tomato and Feta Cheese Sauce

Makes 4 to 6 servings

When it's hot outside, a pasta dish that doesn't have to be served piping hot is refreshing. Just mix uncooked, marinated tomatoes with hot pasta and top with grilled shrimp for a fine dinner. Start a few hours ahead of serving, so the tomatoes have time to give off their juices.

TOMATO SAUCE

2 pounds ripe beefsteak tomatoes
$\frac{1}{4}$ cup olive oil
2 tablespoons chopped fresh oregano or 1 teaspoon dried
1 garlic clove, crushed through a press
$\frac{1}{4}$ teaspoon salt
$\frac{1}{4}$ teaspoon hot red pepper flakes

$1\frac{1}{2}$ pounds extra-large shrimp (21 to 26 per pound), peeled and
    deveined
2 tablespoons olive oil
$\frac{1}{4}$ teaspoon salt
$\frac{1}{4}$ teaspoon freshly ground black pepper
1 pound fettuccine
4 ounces feta cheese, crumbled

1. To make the sauce, mix together the tomatoes, oil, oregano, garlic, salt, and red pepper in a large bowl. Cover and let stand at room temperature until the tomatoes give off some juices, at least 2 hours, and up to 4 hours.

2. Build a charcoal fire in an outdoor grill and let burn until the coals are covered with white ash. **IN A GAS GRILL,** preheat on High.

3. Meanwhile, bring a large pot of lightly salted water to a boil over high heat for the pasta.

4. In a medium bowl, toss the shrimp with the oil, seasoning with the salt and pepper while tossing.

5. Lightly oil the cooking grate. Place the shrimp on the grill and cover. Grill, turning once, until the shrimp are pink and firm, about 5 minutes. Transfer to the bowl of tomatoes.

6. Add the pasta to the boiling water and cook until tender, about 9 minutes or according to the package directions. Drain the pasta and add to the bowl of tomatoes, along with the cheese. Toss well. Serve hot or at room temperature, in individual pasta bowls.

Hawaiian Shrimp and Pineapple Kebabs

FIREFIGHTER MIKE LAVIN AND CAROLINE LAVIN ▪ ENGINE COMPANY 295 ▪
NEW YORK FIRE DEPARTMENT ▪ NEW YORK, NEW YORK

Makes 6 servings

When Mike and Caroline entertain, this is a surefire dinner party hit. Shrimp and pineapple kebabs have been around since backyard parties in the 1950s, but homemade teriyaki sauce and fresh pineapple chunks make it special.

> 36 extra-large shrimp (21 to 26 per pound)
> Teriyaki Marinade (page 63)
> $\frac{1}{2}$ small pineapple, pared and cored, cut into thirty (1-inch) chunks

1. Soak six 12-inch bamboo skewers in water for 30 minutes. Then drain. Combine the shrimp and Teriyaki Marinade in a zippered plastic bag. Close the bag and let stand at room temperature for 30 minutes, no longer. Just before grilling, add the pineapple chunks. Drain.

2. Build a charcoal fire in an outdoor grill and let burn until the coals are covered with white ash. **IN A GAS GRILL,** preheat on High.

3. For each kebab, alternate 6 shrimp and 5 pineapple chunks on each skewer, beginning and ending with a shrimp.

4. Lightly oil the cooking grate. Place the kebabs on the grill and cover. Grill, turning once, until the shrimp are pink and firm, about 5 minutes. Serve immediately.

Beef, Lamb, and Pork

The Classic Grilled Steak

Makes 4 servings

A perfectly grilled steak depends on two things: a good, dry-aged steak and a very hot fire. If you have these two essentials, you don't need to worry about anything else. Marinades and dry rubs are redundant on a fine steak.

Dry-aged steaks are aged for about 3 weeks to develop flavor and tenderness. Supermarket steaks are not well-aged, and while they can be used, they will lack the classic steakhouse flavor. Search out a local butcher who carries these excellent steaks.

If you have real hardwood charcoal (not briquettes), this is the time to use it, as its intense heat will sear the steak beautifully. The coals should be covered with white ash, but be so hot that you can hold your hand at grate level for only 1 or 2 seconds.

Remove the steak from the refrigerator at least 30 minutes before grilling. If you grill a chilled steak, it could end up cold in the center even if it is perfectly browned on the outside.

The fat around the perimeter of the steak should be trimmed to a very thin layer, less than ¼ inch. A little fat will add flavor and moisture, but too much will drip on the coals and create flare-ups. Besides, the fat that gives the steak flavor is marbled throughout the meat, not on the outside. About every 2 inches, notch the fat around the steak with a shallow cut to keep the steak from curling when grilled.

Estimate the cooking time based on the thickness of the steak, not on its weight. A 1-inch-thick steak, regardless of weight, will take 8 minutes to grill to medium-rare over high heat. If your steak is a little thinner, slightly decrease the grilling time.

To tell when your steak is done, try not to cut into it and release all those delicious juices you're trying so hard to retain. The more meat cooks, the more juices evaporate, and the firmer the meat becomes. Professional cooks use the "touch test," which you should master, too. Press the steak (or chop or burger) in the center with a finger. If it is rare, it will feel somewhat squishy, like the fleshy part of your palm when it is relaxed. Medium-done steaks feel somewhat resilient, like the fleshy part of the palm feels when you close your hand gently into a fist. Well-done steaks feel firm, like that area feels when your hand is clenched.

> **4 dry-aged steaks, such as sirloin, shell, T-bone, rib-eye, or Delmonico,
>   cut 1 inch thick**
> **1 teaspoon salt, or to taste**
> **$\frac{1}{2}$ teaspoon freshly ground black pepper, or to taste**

1. 30 minutes to 1 hour before grilling, remove the steaks from the refrigerator.

2. Meanwhile, build a charcoal fire in an outdoor grill and let burn until the coals are covered with white ash. The coals should be very hot—you should be able to hold your hand at grate level for only 1 to 2 seconds. **IN A GAS GRILL,** preheat on High.

3. Just before grilling, season the steaks with the salt and pepper. (I allow about $\frac{1}{4}$ teaspoon salt and $\frac{1}{8}$ teaspoon pepper per steak.) Lightly oil the cooking grate. Place the steaks on the grill and cover. Cook, turning once, until the steaks are well-browned on the exterior, but medium-rare within, about 8 minutes. If you like your steak more well done, move it to the cooler, outer perimeter of the charcoal, not directly over the coals. Turning the steaks once again, continue grilling, covered, for about 3 more minutes for medium-done steak, and 5 more minutes for well-done. **IN A GAS GRILL,** reduce the heat to Medium, and continue grilling for approximately the same time periods as for charcoal.

Tuscan T-Bone Steaks

Makes 4 servings

In Tuscany, a massive T-bone steak is grilled over oak wood and served with nothing but a drizzle of the best olive oil with salt and pepper. We can make do here with our own beef, which is pretty darned good, too, cut to manageable proportions. An oak wood fire takes too long to burn down, so sprinkle your hardwood charcoal or briquette coals with soaked and drained oak chips to give your T-bone authentic Florentine flavor.

> Four 1¼-pound T-bone steaks, cut about 1 inch thick
> 1½ tablespoons extra-virgin olive oil, plus additional for serving
> 1 teaspoon salt
> ½ teaspoon freshly ground black pepper
> Lemon wedges

1. Brush both sides of each steak with the olive oil. Let stand at room temperature for 1 hour.

2. Meanwhile, build a charcoal fire in an outdoor grill and let burn until covered with white ash. The coals should be very hot—you should be able to hold your hand at grate level for only 1 to 2 seconds. **IN A GAS GRILL,** preheat on High.

3. Just before grilling, season the steaks with the salt and pepper. Lightly oil the cooking grate. Place the steaks on the grill and cover. Cook, turning once, until the steaks are well-browned on the exterior and rare within, 6 to 8 minutes. (Tuscans prefer very rare steak, but cook it to your taste.) If you like your steak more well done, move it to the cooler, outer perimeter of the charcoal, not directly over the coals. Turning the steaks once again, continue grilling, covered, for about 3 more minutes for medium-done steaks, and 5 more minutes for well-done. **IN A GAS GRILL,** reduce the heat to medium, and continue grilling for approximately the same time as for charcoal. Serve immediately, with the lemon wedges and a cruet of olive oil for seasoning at the table.

Gaucho-Style Steaks

Makes 4 servings

Argentina is renown for its "beef culture," which includes world-class steak-houses in Buenos Aires, and their own brand of cowboy, called the *gaucho*. They even have their own brand of steak sauce: a vinegary onion brew called *chimichurri*.

> Four 14-ounce shell (also called New York or boneless club) steaks,
>   cut about 1 inch thick
> $1\frac{1}{2}$ tablespoons olive oil
> 2 teaspoons dried oregano
> 1 teaspoon salt
> $\frac{1}{2}$ teaspoon freshly ground black pepper
> Argentine Steak Sauce (page 79)

1. Brush both sides of each steak with the olive oil. Rub with the oregano. Let stand at room temperature for 1 hour.

2. Meanwhile, build a charcoal fire in an outdoor grill and let burn until covered with white ash. The coals should be very hot—you should be able to hold your hand at grate level for only 1 to 2 seconds. **IN A GAS GRILL,** preheat on High.

3. Just before grilling, season the steaks with the salt and pepper. Lightly oil the cooking grate. Place the steaks on the grill and cover. Cook, turning once, until the steaks are well-browned on the exterior and medium-rare within, about 8 minutes. If you like your steak more well done, move it to the cooler, outer perimeter of the charcoal, not directly over the coals. Turning the steaks once again, continue grilling, covered, for about 3 more minutes for medium-done steaks, and 5 more minutes for well-done. **IN A GAS GRILL,** reduce the heat to medium, and continue grilling for approximately the same time as for charcoal. Serve immediately, with the sauce passed on the side.

Steak and Arugula Salad

**FIREFIGHTER EDWARD MARTIN ▪ LADDER COMPANY 152 ▪
NEW YORK FIRE DEPARTMENT ▪ NEW YORK, NEW YORK**

Makes 4 servings

Ed is one of FDNY's best cooks. This is his easy one-dish meal for a summer supper. The marinade does double-duty as a dressing. Be sure to rinse the arugula well, as it can hide sand in its curly leaves.

$\frac{1}{2}$ cup hearty red wine, such as zinfandel
2 tablespoons red wine vinegar
2 garlic cloves, crushed through a press
$\frac{1}{2}$ teaspoon salt
$\frac{1}{4}$ freshly ground black pepper
1 cup olive oil, preferably extra-virgin
One 1$\frac{1}{2}$-pound sirloin steak, cut about $\frac{3}{4}$ inch thick
12 ounces arugula, thick stems removed, torn into bite-sized pieces
2 ripe beefsteak tomatoes, sliced

1. In a medium bowl, whisk together the wine, vinegar, garlic, salt, and pepper. Gradually whisk in the oil. Pour $\frac{1}{2}$ cup of the dressing into a zippered plastic bag and add the steak. Let the steak stand at room temperature for 1 hour. (Or refrigerate for up to 4 hours, and remove from the refrigerator 1 hour before grilling.) Cover and refrigerate the remaining dressing.

2. Build a charcoal fire in an outdoor grill and let burn until the coals are covered with white ash. The coals should be very hot—you should be able to hold your hand at grate level for only 1 to 2 seconds. **IN A GAS GRILL,** preheat on High.

3. Lightly oil the cooking grate. Place the steak on the grill and cover the grill. Cook, turning once, until the steak is well-browned on the exterior and medium-rare within, 6 to 8 minutes. If you like your steak more well done, move it to the cooler, outer perimeter of the charcoal, not directly over the coals. Turning the steaks once again, continue grilling, covered, for about 3 more minutes for medium-done steaks, and 5 more minutes for well-done. **IN A GAS GRILL,**

reduce the heat to medium, and continue grilling for approximately the same time as for charcoal.

4. Transfer the steak to a cutting board and let stand for 3 minutes. Cut the steak on the diagonal into $\frac{1}{4}$-inch-thick slices (cutting on the diagonal gives wider slices.)

5. Place the arugula on a large deep serving platter and toss with the remaining dressing. Top with the sliced steak and tomatoes, pouring any carving juices over the steak. Serve immediately.

Grilled Steak Fajitas with Guaca-Salsa-Mole

Makes 6 servings

Skirt steak is the first choice for fajitas, but flank steak is a fine substitute. To serve family-style, place the steak, grilled vegetables, and Guaca-Salsa-Mole in individual bowls, and pass a basket of warm tortillas alongside, allowing everyone to make their own fajitas to their liking.

$\frac{1}{3}$ cup fresh lime juice
1 tablespoon chili powder
1 teaspoon ground cumin
1 garlic clove, crushed through a press
$\frac{1}{4}$ teaspoon salt
$\frac{1}{2}$ cup olive oil
$1\frac{1}{2}$ pounds skirt steak, trimmed
1 large onion, cut into $\frac{1}{4}$-inch-thick rings
2 medium bell peppers (1 red, 1 green), seeded and cut into
    $\frac{1}{4}$-inch-thick rings
Twelve 8-inch flour tortillas
Guaca-Salsa-Mole (page 26)

1. In a medium bowl, whisk together the lime juice, chili powder, cumin, garlic, and salt. Gradually whisk in the oil. Place the steak, marinade, onion, and peppers in a zippered plastic bag. Close the bag and refrigerate, turning the bag occasionally, for at least 1 hour, and up to 4 hours.

2. Build a charcoal fire in an outdoor grill and let burn until covered with white ash. The coals should be very hot—you should be able to hold your hand at grate level for only 1 to 2 seconds. **IN A GAS GRILL,** preheat on High.

3. Stack 6 tortillas and wrap in aluminum foil. Repeat with the remaining tortillas. Remove the onion and pepper rings from the marinade and place on a lightly oiled vegetable grilling grate or a sheet of aluminum foil. Drain the steak, but do not pat dry.

4. Lightly oil the cooking grate. Place the vegetables, still on the grilling grate or foil, on the grill and cover. Grill the vegetables for 5 minutes. Using a wide spatula, turn the vegetables. Place the steak on the grill and cover. Grill, turning the steak once, until the steak is well-browned on the exterior and medium-rare within and the vegetables are tender, 7 to 9 minutes. During the last 5 minutes, add the wrapped tortillas to the grill to heat through.

5. Transfer the steak to a cutting board and the vegetables to a bowl. Using a very sharp, thin-bladed knife, cut the steak on the diagonal into $1/4$-inch-thick slices. Wrap the sliced steak and grilled vegetables with a dollop of the Guaca-Salsa-Mole in each tortilla. Serve immediately.

Asian Flank Steak with
Napa Cabbage and Pineapple Slaw

Makes 4 to 6 servings

When you want marinated steak, nothing beats flank steak. (Lately, other cuts of meat are being labeled as "London broil," but they don't end up as moist and flavorful as flank.) This recipe uses the classic teriyaki marinade, but it gets an update with its unusual slaw.

> One 1$^3/_4$-pound flank steak, trimmed
> Teriyaki Marinade (page 63)
> Napa Cabbage and Pineapple Slaw (page 34)

1. Place the flank steak and marinade in a zippered plastic bag. Let stand at room temperature for 1 hour.

2. Build a charcoal fire in an outdoor grill and let burn until covered with white ash. The coals should be very hot—you should be able to hold your hand at grate level for only 1 to 2 seconds. **IN A GAS GRILL,** preheat on High.

3. Drain the steak, but do not pat dry. Lightly oil the cooking grate. Place the steak on the grill and cover. Cook, turning once, until well-browned on the exterior and medium-rare within, 7 to 9 minutes.

4. Transfer the steak to a cutting board. Using a very sharp, thin-bladed knife, cut the steak on the diagonal into $^1/_4$-inch-thick slices. Place the slaw on a large platter, top with the steak slices, and pour any carving juices over all. Serve immediately.

The Classic Marinated Beef Tenderloin

CAPTAIN TOM MITCHELL ▪ LADDER COMPANY 152 ▪
NEW YORK FIRE DEPARTMENT ▪ NEW YORK, NEW YORK

Makes 8 to 10 servings

My captain for the last few years is a sworn red-meat eater, so we try to accommodate him as much as we can. When the captain is happy, the rest of the firehouse is happy. Beef tenderloin is one of the most tender cuts, and its lean, beefy flavor makes it worth the cost.

One 4-pound beef tenderloin
Tuscan Red Wine Marinade (page 59)

1. Place the beef and the marinade in a shallow baking dish and cover. Refrigerate for at least 2 hours, and up to 8 hours, turning the beef occasionally. Remove from the refrigerator 1 hour before grilling.

2. Build a charcoal fire (use about 4 pounds of briquettes) on one side of an outdoor grill and let burn until covered with white ash. Place a disposable aluminum foil pan on the empty side of the grill, and fill halfway with water. **IN A GAS GRILL,** preheat on High. Turn one burner off, leaving the other burner(s) on High. Place a large disposable aluminum foil pan over the Off burner and fill halfway with water.

3. Remove the beef from the marinade and pat dry with paper towels. Fold back the pointed tip of the tenderloin, and tie it to the roast so the roast is the same thickness throughout its length. Tie the tenderloin crosswise and lengthwise with kitchen twine.

4. Lightly oil the cooking grate. Place the tenderloin over the coals and cover. Grill, turning occasionally, until seared on all sides, about 10 minutes. Move the tenderloin over the pan. **IN A GAS GRILL,** grill over High burner, turning occasionally, until seared on all sides, about 10 minutes. Move the tenderloin to the Off burner.

continued

5. Continue roasting until an instant-read thermometer inserted in the center of the roast reads 130° F for medium-rare meat, about 20 minutes. Check the meat's temperature frequently to avoid overcooking.

6. Let the tenderloin stand for 5 minutes before removing the twine. Carve crosswise into ½-inch-thick slices and serve.

Smokehouse Beef Brisket with Can-of-Suds Basting Sauce

LT. THOMAS FINNERTY ▪ ENGINE COMPANY 299 ▪ NEW YORK FIRE DEPARTMENT ▪ NEW YORK CITY, NEW YORK

Makes 6 to 8 servings

Smoke, although deadly to firefighters, adds delicious flavor to grilled foods. After working a few fires, my fellow firefighters and I feel just like the recipe—smoked to the core. It can take days to remove the smoke aroma from your skin and hair. This excellent brisket uses beer to keep the beef moist, and I don't know many off-duty firefighters who don't love beer. I got this recipe from Lt. Finnerty, who not only is a marathon runner and an avid cyclist, but is also such a fan of fine food and drink that he brews his own beer.

> One 5½-pound first-cut beef brisket, trimmed to leave a ¼-inch layer of fat
> 2 tablespoons canola oil
> 2 tablespoons chili powder
> Classic BBQ Sauce (page 74)
>
> **CAN-OF-SUDS BASTING SAUCE**
>
> 1 tablespoon vegetable oil
> 1 medium onion, chopped
> 2 garlic cloves, chopped

One 12-ounce can lager beer

$\frac{1}{4}$ cup cider vinegar

2 tablespoons spicy brown mustard

2 tablespoons ketchup

1 tablespoon Worcestershire sauce

1 teaspoon salt

4 cups mesquite chips, soaked in water for at least 30 minutes, and drained

1. Brush the brisket with the oil and rub with the chili powder. Let stand at room temperature for 1 hour before smoking.

2. To make the basting sauce, heat the oil in a medium saucepan over medium heat. Add the onion and garlic and cook until softened, about 4 minutes. Add the beer, vinegar, mustard, ketchup, Worcestershire sauce, and salt and bring to a boil. Reduce the heat to low and simmer for 20 minutes.

3. Build a charcoal fire on one side of an outdoor grill and let burn until covered with white ash. The fire should be medium-hot—you should be able to hold your hand at grate level for only 3 seconds. Place a large disposable aluminum foil pan on the other side of the grill and fill halfway with water. Sprinkle the coals with a handful of drained chips. **IN A GAS GRILL,** preheat on High. Turn one burner off, and the other burner(s) to Low. Place a large disposable aluminum pan on the Off burner and fill halfway with water. Place a handful of chips in the metal chip box. Or, wrap a handful of chips in aluminum foil, pierce a few holes in the foil, and place the foil packet on the heat source.

4. Lightly oil the cooking grate. Place the brisket over the pan, fat side up, and cover the grill. Smoke the brisket for 5 to 6 hours until very tender and a meat thermometer inserted in the thickest part reads 165° F. About every 40 minutes, baste well with the basting sauce, and add more ignited coals and chips to maintain a temperature of about 300° F. (If your grill doesn't have a thermostat on its lid, place an oven thermometer next to the brisket to get a reading.) **IN A GAS GRILL,** add more chips or foil packets at the same time as basting.

5. Let the brisket stand for 10 minutes, then slice thinly across the grain. Serve with the barbecue sauce passed on the side.

Garlicky Smoked Prime Rib

Makes 8 to 10 servings

Beware: Once you have served prime rib cooked this way, your friends will never want it any other way. You won't be able to serve the pan juices (they will be overly smoky and may have ashes from the coals), but the meat will be so juicy and delicious, no one will miss them.

> One 6-pound boneless rib roast
> 2 tablespoons olive oil
> 1½ teaspoons salt
> 1 teaspoon coarsely cracked black peppercorns (crushed in a mortar or under a heavy skillet)
> 6 garlic cloves
> 4 cups oak or mesquite chips, soaked in water for 30 minutes, and drained

1. Using a sharp knife, cut the fat "cap" from the roast in one piece. Cut just where the fat is attached to the meat, trimming off as little meat as possible. Reserve the fat cap. Brush the meat with 1 tablespoon of the oil. Season with 1 teaspoon of the salt and the cracked pepper.

2. On a work surface, finely chop the garlic cloves. Sprinkle with the remaining ½ teaspoon salt. Chop and smear the garlic on the work surface until it forms a paste. In a small bowl, mix the garlic paste with the remaining 1 tablespoon oil. Spread the garlic mixture over the area where the fat cap was cut. Replace the fat cap and tie it back onto the roast with kitchen twine. Let the roast stand at room temperature for 1 hour.

3. Meanwhile, build a charcoal fire (use about 4 pounds of briquettes) on one side of an outdoor grill and let burn until covered with white ash. Place a large disposable aluminum foil pan on the other side of the grill and fill halfway with water. Sprinkle a handful of chips over the coals. **IN A GAS GRILL,** preheat on High. Turn one burner off, and adjust the other burner(s) to Medium. Place a disposable aluminum foil pan on the Off burner and fill halfway with water.

Place a handful of chips in the metal chip box. Or, wrap a handful of chips in aluminum foil, pierce a few holes in the foil, and place the packet on the heat source.

4. Lightly oil the cooking grate. Place the roast over the pan, fat side up, and cover the grill. Cook for 2 to 2½ hours, until a meat thermometer inserted in the thickest part of the roast reads 130° F for medium-rare meat (allowing approximately 20 minutes per pound). About every 45 minutes, add more ignited coals and wood chips as needed to maintain a grill temperature of about 325° F. (If your grill doesn't have a thermostat on its lid, place an oven thermometer next to the roast to get a reading.) **IN A GAS GRILL,** just add more chips or foil packets every 30 minutes.

5. Let the roast stand for 10 minutes before removing the twine and fat. Carve and serve immediately.

"Joan of Arc" BBQ Short Ribs

**FIREFIGHTER MARK MALENOVSKY ▪ ENGINE COMPANY 299 ▪
NEW YORK FIRE DEPARTMENT ▪ NEW YORK, NEW YORK**

Makes 4 to 6 servings

These ribs got their name for the number of times Mark has burned them.
It's (usually) not his fault! One of the things that makes firehouse cooking
unique is trying to cook between alarms. It can be tough to time the meals,
especially grilled ones, and our suppers often end up on the burned side—
just like Joan of Arc. Short ribs are tasty, but they need to be simmered in
liquid to be tender. This grilling method does the trick, as long as no alarms
go off.

> Eight 12-ounce beef short ribs
> 1 teaspoon salt
> $\frac{1}{2}$ teaspoon freshly ground black pepper
> 1 cup lager beer
> 2 cups Cup-of-Joe BBQ Sauce (page 75)

1. Season the ribs with salt and pepper. Tear off eight 12-inch squares of aluminum foil. Place 1 rib in the center of a square. Add 2 tablespoons beer and 1
tablespoon barbecue sauce. Fold up the sides to enclose the rib and liquids. Repeat with the remaining ribs, beer, and sauce, setting aside the remaining sauce
for glazing the ribs later.

2. Build a charcoal fire in an outdoor grill and let burn until the coals are covered with white ash. Leave the coals heaped in a mound. Do not spread them
out. **IN A GAS GRILL,** preheat on High. Adjust the temperature to Medium.

3. Place the wrapped ribs on the cooler, outside perimeter of the grill, not directly over the coals, and cover. Cook, without turning, until the short ribs are
tender (open a packet to check), about $1\frac{1}{4}$ hours. The fire will burn down, but
don't add more coals. **IN A GAS GRILL,** cover the grill and cook the wrapped ribs
over Medium heat. Unwrap the ribs, discard the cooking liquid, and set them

aside. (The ribs can be prepared up to 1 hour ahead, covered, and kept at room temperature.)

4. Add more charcoal to the fire and let it burn until the coals are covered with white ash again. Spread out the coals into an even layer. **IN A GAS GRILL,** increase the heat to High.

5. Lightly oil the cooking grate. Place the ribs on the grill. Cook, turning occasionally and basting with the barbecue sauce, until the ribs are hot and glazed, about 10 minutes. Serve immediately, with any remaining sauce passed on the side.

The Classic Grilled Burger

Makes 4 servings

There are a few secrets to a really great burger—one that is thick and juicy, and tastes like a burger no matter how much ketchup and relish you put on it. First, you must use ground round (85% lean) beef. Ground chuck is too fatty, and ground sirloin is too lean. Don't compact the burgers by overhandling when making the patties, or they will turn out dry. And finally, never press down on the burger while it's cooking. Why would anyone want to squeeze out the juices?

> 1⅓ pounds ground round (85% lean) beef
> 1 teaspoon salt
> ¼ teaspoon freshly ground black pepper
> 4 hamburger buns, split
> Ketchup, mustard, mayonnaise, sliced onion, hamburger relish,
>   lettuce leaves, and sliced tomatoes

1. Build a charcoal fire in an outdoor grill and let burn until the coals are covered with white ash. **IN A GAS GRILL,** preheat on High.

2. In a medium bowl, combine the ground round, salt, and pepper. Lightly form the mixture into 4 burgers about 4 inches in diameter.

3. Lightly oil the cooking grate. Place the burgers on the grill and cover. Grill, turning once, until the outside is well-browned but the inside is still pink and juicy, about 8 minutes for medium-rare burgers. If you like your burgers more well-done, move the burgers to the cooler, outer perimeter of the grill, not directly over the coals. Turn the burgers, cover, and continue cooking for about 2 more minutes for medium burgers, or about 4 more minutes for well-done burgers. **IN A GAS GRILL,** reduce the heat to Medium, and continue cooking the burgers for approximately the same time periods. During the last 2 minutes, place the buns on the grill to toast.

4. Place the burgers in the buns and let everyone choose their own fixings.

Stuffed Cheeseburgers

Makes 4 servings

Why make regular cheeseburgers when you can make stuffed cheeseburgers?

> 1⅓ pounds ground round (85% lean) beef
> 2 tablespoons bottled steak sauce
> 1 teaspoon salt
> ¼ teaspoon freshly ground black pepper
> 1 cup shredded sharp Cheddar cheese
> 4 hamburger buns, split
> Ketchup, mustard, mayonnaise, sliced onion, hamburger relish,
>   lettuce leaves, and sliced tomatoes

1. Build a charcoal fire in an outdoor grill and let burn until the coals are covered with white ash. **IN A GAS GRILL,** preheat on High.

2. In a medium bowl, mix the ground round, steak sauce, salt, and pepper. Lightly form the mixture into 8 thin burgers about 4 inches in diameter. Mound 2 tablespoons shredded cheese on 4 burgers, top each with a second burger, and pinch the edges shut to seal the cheese inside the meat.

3. Lightly oil the cooking grate. Place the burgers on the grill and cover. Grill, turning once, until the outside is well-browned but the inside is still pink and juicy, about 8 minutes for medium-rare burgers. If you like your burgers more well-done, move the burgers to the cooler, outer perimeter of the grill, not directly over the coals. Turn the burgers, cover, and continue cooking for about 2 more minutes for medium burgers, or about 4 more minutes for well-done burgers. **IN A GAS GRILL,** reduce the heat to Medium, and continue cooking the burgers for approximately the same time periods. During the last 2 minutes, sprinkle the remaining cheese on the burgers and place the buns on the grill to toast.

4. Place the burgers in the buns and let everyone choose their own fixings.

Burgers Italiano

**FIREFIGHTER LOUIS MINUTOLI ▪ LADDER COMPANY 129 ▪
NEW YORK FIRE DEPARTMENT ▪ NEW YORK, NEW YORK**

Makes 4 servings

Louie is one of Ladder 129's best cooks, and appeared with me on "Live with
Regis and Kathie Lee." This fine and simple recipe mixes some classic Italian ingredients and is one of Louie's best.

12 ounces ground round (85% lean) beef
8 ounces sweet Italian sausage, casing removed
$^1/_3$ cup pitted and chopped black brine-cured olives
1 teaspoon Italian Herb Rub (page 69) or Italian herb seasoning
$^3/_4$ teaspoon salt
$^1/_4$ teaspoon freshly ground black pepper
$^1/_2$ cup bottled pizza sauce
4 slices mozzarella cheese
Four 4-inch squares of focaccia, split, or 4 hamburger buns

1. Build a charcoal fire in an outdoor grill and let burn until the coals are covered with white ash. **IN A GAS GRILL,** preheat on High.

2. In a medium bowl, working as quickly and gently as possible, mix the ground beef, sausage, olives, Italian seasonings, salt, and pepper. Lightly form into 4 patties about 1 inch thick. Warm the pizza sauce in a small saucepan on the edge of the grill.

3. Lightly oil the cooking grate. Place the burgers on the grill and cover. Grill, turning once, until the outside is well-browned, but the inside is still pink and juicy, 8 to 10 minutes for medium-rare burgers. If you like your burgers more well-done, move the burgers to the cooler, outer perimeter of the grill, not directly over the coals. Turn the burgers, cover, and continue cooking for about 2 more minutes for medium burgers, or about 4 more minutes for well-done burgers. **IN A GAS GRILL,** reduce the heat to Medium, and continue cooking the burgers for approximately the same time periods. During the last 2 minutes, top each burger with a slice of mozzarella, and place the focaccia on the grill to heat through.

4. Brush the cut sides of the focaccia with the pizza sauce. Make sandwiches out of the focaccia and burgers and serve immediately.

The Classic Butterflied Leg of Lamb

**FIREFIGHTER AMNON SZANTO ▪ ENGINE COMPANY 299 ▪
NEW YORK FIRE DEPARTMENT ▪ NEW YORK CITY, NEW YORK**

Makes 6 to 8 servings

Amnon is a New York firefighter from Israel, where lamb is very popular. (We started our careers together in the same firehouse, Engine 319. It's a co-incidence that we are in another firehouse now that our careers are winding down.)

Grilled butterflied leg of lamb is popular in America, too, but it isn't problem-free. A whole leg of lamb, once boned, is thick in some places, and thin in others. To some cooks, that's okay, because they end up with lamb cooked to different degrees of doneness, so everyone can get what they prefer. But it's really better to prepare the lamb so it is somewhat the same thickness and can be grilled to the same doneness throughout.

First, ask your butcher to bone a leg of lamb for you. Do not be a hero and try to do it yourself, as the lamb bone structure is intricate, especially at the hip joint, and it calls for a professional's expertise. Ask the butcher to trim away all of the surface fat. A whole 9- to 10-pound leg of lamb will weigh about 5½ pounds after boning, serving around 10 people. For smaller meals, use a 5-pound leg of lamb to get about 2½ pounds of boneless leg of lamb. Whether you use the butt or shank end is up to you—the butt looks meatier, but actually has a lot of bones. If you are the kind of cook who likes to make soup, ask the butcher to saw the bones into 2-inch pieces, and use them to make a broth (it is great for lentil or split pea soup).

Many of the marinades in this book are lamb-friendly. Zinfandel-Mint Marinade has the most classic flavors, but also try the Tandoori Marinade (page 64) or Tuscan Red Wine Marinade (page 59).

One 5½-pound boneless leg of lamb
Zinfandel-Mint Marinade (page 60)

1. Place the boned lamb on your work counter, smooth side down, with the lamb positioned horizontally. Cut the lamb vertically into two roasts, as equally sized as possible. On each roast, use a sharp knife to cut a deep, vertical, 70° incision into the thickest part of the meat to make a flap—don't cut all the way through the meat. Open up this flap of meat like a book. Continue making a few more incisions, opening up the flaps as you go, until the meat is of even thickness.

2. Place the lamb in a zippered plastic bag and add the marinade. Refrigerate for at least 2 hours, or up to overnight. Remove from the refrigerator 1 hour before grilling.

3. Build a charcoal fire in an outdoor grill and let burn until covered with white ash. Bank the coals into a mound that is about 3 coals deep on one end, sloping to 1 coal deep on the opposite end. **IN A GAS GRILL,** preheat on High.

4. Lightly oil the cooking grate. Place the two lamb roasts on the grill over the hot, deep end of the coal mound and cover. Grill, turning once, until browned on both sides, about 10 minutes. Transfer to the cooler, shallow end of the coal mound. **IN A GAS GRILL,** grill over High heat, turning occasionally, until browned on both sides, about 10 minutes. Reduce the heat to Medium.

5. Grill until an instant-read thermometer inserted in a thick part of the roast reads 130° for medium-rare lamb, 15 to 20 minutes more.

6. Transfer to a carving board and let stand for 5 minutes before slicing across the grain.

"Burned Fingers" Lamb Rib Chops

Makes 4 servings

In Rome, these are called *scottaditto* meaning "burn fingers," which is what happens when you eat these the Roman way, held by the bone and nibbled. This is a fantastic way to prepare lamb chops, but be careful not to overcook them—they're thin and only take a few minutes. I'd serve these with Grilled Asparagus and Grilled New Potatoes (pages 46 and 48).

8 lamb rib chops, cut about $1/2$ inch thick
2 tablespoons olive oil
1 teaspoon crumbed dried rosemary
$3/4$ teaspoon salt
$1/2$ teaspoon hot red pepper flakes
Lemon wedges

1. Using a sharp knife, scrape the meat from the bone end of each chop to make a bone "handle." Using a meat mallet, pound the meaty part of each chop to flatten slightly. Brush the chops with the olive oil and season with the rosemary, salt, and red pepper flakes. Cover and let stand for 1 hour at room temperature.

2. Build a charcoal fire in an outdoor grill and let burn until covered with white ash. **IN A GAS GRILL,** preheat on High.

3. Lightly oil the cooking grate. Place the chops on the grill. Grill, uncovered, turning once, until seared on both sides, about 5 minutes for medium rare. Serve hot, with the lemon wedges.

Grilled Mini-Lamb Burgers in Pitas

Makes 6 servings

These spiced lamb burgers will remind you of a Greek gyro. If your butcher doesn't carry ground lamb, ask to have it freshly ground from a well-trimmed leg of lamb.

$1\frac{1}{3}$ pounds lean ground lamb
$\frac{1}{2}$ cup dried breadcrumbs
1 medium onion, shredded on the large holes of a box grater
1 garlic clove, crushed through a press
1 teaspoon ground cumin
$1\frac{1}{4}$ teaspoons salt
$\frac{1}{2}$ teaspoon freshly ground black pepper
1 pickling (Kirby) cucumber, scrubbed, seeded, and thinly sliced
3 plum tomatoes, thinly sliced
1 small red onion, minced
$\frac{2}{3}$ cup plain low-fat yogurt
1 teaspoon dried oregano
6 pita breads, tops cut off to form pockets

1. Build a charcoal fire in an outdoor grill and let burn until the coals are covered with white ash. **IN A GAS GRILL,** preheat on High.

2. In a medium bowl, working as quickly and lightly as possible, combine the ground lamb, breadcrumbs, grated onion, garlic, cumin, salt, and pepper. Using a heaping tablespoon for each, form into 24 patties about $^3/_4$ inch thick.

3. In a medium bowl, combine the cucumber, tomatoes, and red onion. In a small bowl, mix the yogurt and oregano. Set the bowls aside.

4. Lightly oil the cooking grate. Place the patties on the grill and cover. Grill, turning once, until the patties are medium-rare, about 4 minutes. During the last minute or so, place the pitas on the grill to heat through.

5. Fill each pita with 3 or 4 patties, about $^1/_4$ cup of the vegetable mixture, and a spoonful of the yogurt sauce. Serve immediately.

The Best BBQ Ribs

CAPTAIN PHILIP PARR ▪ ENGINE COMPANY 299 ▪ NEW YORK FIRE DEPARTMENT ▪ NEW YORK, NEW YORK

Makes 4 to 6 servings

Captain Parr claims to make the best ribs, period. Real barbecued ribs are slow-cooked (it can take up to 24 hours in a slow smokehouse smoker) and are never cooked over coals. At the firehouse, we don't have that kind of time, so we combine the best of many different outdoor cooking techniques to make these championship ribs. Note that this is a two-step method, and shows how a good grill cook controls his or her fire to get the best results. First, the ribs are wrapped in foil and grilled so they can cook in their own juices and render off most of the fat. As the fire will have burned down during this first step, more coals are added to the grill to build a second fire for glazing the ribs. But, let this second fire burn down to medium-hot heat, so the ribs won't burn when glazed with the sweet BBQ sauce.

> 5 pounds pork spareribs, cut into slabs
> $\frac{1}{3}$ cup Lone Star Dry Rub (page 70)
> $1\frac{1}{2}$ cups mesquite or hickory wood chips, soaked in water for
>   30 minutes, and drained.
> 2 cups Classic BBQ Sauce (page 74)

1. Rub the spareribs with the dry rub. Wrap each slab tightly in a double thickness of aluminum foil. Set aside while building the fire.

2. Build a charcoal fire in an outdoor grill and let burn until the coals are covered with white ash. **IN A GAS GRILL,** preheat on High, then adjust to Low.

3. Place the foil-wrapped ribs on the grill and cover. Cook, turning occasionally, until the ribs are tender, about 1 hour. Unwrap the ribs and set aside.

4. Add more charcoal to the fire and let burn until medium-hot. You should be able to hold your hand at grill level for about 3 seconds. Sprinkle the drained chips over the coals. **IN A GAS GRILL,** keep the heat on Low. Place the drained chips in the metal chip box. Or, wrap the chips in aluminum foil, pierce a few holes in the foil, and place on the heat source.

5. Lightly oil the cooking grate. Place the ribs on the grill, brush with sauce, and cover. Grill for 5 minutes. Turn, brush with more sauce. Cover and continue grilling until the ribs are glazed, about 5 more minutes.

6. Cut between the bones into individual ribs. Serve hot, with any remaining sauce passed on the side.

Oak-Smoked Ribs with Italian Herb Rub

CHIEF ALAN BRUNACINI ▪ **PHOENIX FIRE DEPARTMENT** ▪ **PHOENIX, ARIZONA**

Makes 4 to 6 servings

Chief Brunacini, of Phoenix's fire department, holds an annual Health and Safety Symposium, to which he invited me as a guest speaker. He is very concerned about the health of his firefighters, and his department is one of the fittest in the world. Chief "Bruno" also loves to eat, and here is one of his favorites—Italian-style ribs.

> 5 pounds pork spareribs, cut into slabs
> Italian Herb Rub (page 69)
> 3 cups oak chips, soaked in water for 30 minutes and drained

1. Build a charcoal fire on one side of an outdoor grill and let burn until covered with white ash. Place a large disposable aluminum foil pan on the other side of the grill and fill halfway with water. **IN A GAS GRILL,** preheat the grill on High. Turn one burner off, and adjust the other burner(s) to Medium. Place a large disposable aluminum foil pan over the Off burner and fill halfway with water.

2. Smear the herb rub all over the ribs.

3. Lightly oil the cooking grate. Place the ribs over the pan, fat side up, overlapping as needed. Sprinkle a handful of drained chips over the coals and cover. **IN A GAS GRILL,** place the drained chips in the metal chip box. Or, wrap the chips in aluminum foil, pierce a few holes in the foil, and place on the heat source. Cover the grill.

4. Cook until the ribs are very tender, about 2 hours. Every 30 minutes, turn the ribs and add additional ignited coals and a handful of chips to maintain a temperature of about 300° F. **IN A GAS GRILL,** just add more chips or foil packets about every 30 minutes. (If your grill doesn't have a thermostat on its lid, place an oven thermometer next to the ribs to get a reading.)

5. Chop between the bones into individual ribs, and serve hot.

Classic BBQ Ribs Instead of the herb-garlic mixture, use $\frac{1}{3}$ cup Lone Star Dry Rub (page 70). Substitute mesquite or hickory for the oak wood chips. During the last 20 minutes of cooking, turn and brush the ribs occasionally with Classic BBQ Sauce (page 74). Serve, with additional sauce passed on the side.

Greg's Slow-Cooked Ribs

FIREFIGHTER GREG WEBER ▪ LINDEN FIRE DEPARTMENT ▪ LINDEN, NEW JERSEY

Makes 4 to 6 servings

Greg proves that there's more than one way to get great ribs. His method of braising the ribs on the grill in a covered pan gives tender results. It is much better than those recipes that instruct you to boil or bake the ribs first. He uses a gas grill, which means that the heat is easy to adjust so the braising liquid simmers. If you use a charcoal grill, let the coals burn down to medium before placing the pan over them, add a few ignited coals every 30 minutes to maintain the heat, and add water to the pan if the liquid boils away.

> 2 cups Fire-Eater's Sauce (page 78)
> 1 large onion, quartered
> 1 medium carrot, coarsely chopped
> 1 medium celery rib, coarsely chopped
> 2 garlic cloves, crushed under a knife
> 5 pounds pork spareribs, cut into slabs
> $1\frac{1}{2}$ teaspoons salt
> $\frac{1}{2}$ teaspoon freshly ground black pepper

1. Build a charcoal fire in an outdoor grill and let burn until the coals are covered with white ash. The fire should be medium hot—you should be able to hold your hand at grate level for 3 seconds. **IN A GAS GRILL,** preheat on High, then adjust to Medium-Low.

2. In a large disposable aluminum pan, mix $1\frac{1}{2}$ cups water with $\frac{1}{2}$ cup of the sauce and the onion, carrot, celery, and garlic. Season the spareribs with the salt and pepper. Place in the pan, turn to coat with the sauce mixture, and cover tightly with aluminum foil.

3. Place the pan on the cooking grate and cover. Grill, checking occasionally to be sure the liquid doesn't boil away, and adding more water as needed, until the ribs are very tender, about 2 hours. Add a few ignited coals to the charcoal grill every 30 minutes to maintain the heat. Turn the ribs halfway through grilling. Remove the ribs from the pan and set aside. Discard the contents of the pan.

4. Add more coals to a charcoal grill and let burn until covered with white ash. **IN A GAS GRILL,** increase the heat to High, cover, and heat for 10 minutes. Lightly oil the cooking grate. Grill the ribs, turning occasionally, until browned, about 5 minutes.

5. Cut between the bones into individual ribs. Serve hot, with the remaining sauce served on the side.

Pork Roast, Carolina BBQ-Style

Makes 6 servings

In North Carolina, barbecue means hickory-smoked pork with a vinegar sauce. No matter where you live, here's a marinated pork to recall the traditional flavor of Carolina "Q."

CAROLINA BBQ SOP

$1\frac{1}{4}$ cups cider vinegar
4 tablespoons ($\frac{1}{2}$ stick) unsalted butter
$\frac{1}{4}$ cup vegetable oil
2 garlic cloves, finely chopped
1 teaspoon hot red pepper flakes
1 teaspoon salt

3 to $3\frac{1}{2}$ pounds rolled boneless pork roast
2 cups hickory chips, soaked in water for 30 minutes and drained

1. To make the sop, combine all of the ingredients in a medium saucepan with $\frac{1}{2}$ cup water. Bring to a simmer over low heat and simmer for 10 minutes. Cool completely.

2. In a large glass or stainless steel bowl, combine the pork roast and sop. Cover and marinate in the refrigerator, turning occasionally, for at least 2 hours, and up to 4 hours. Remove from the refrigerator 1 hour before cooking.

3. Build a charcoal fire (use about 4 pounds of briquettes) in an outdoor grill on one side of the grill and let burn until covered with white ash. Put a large disposable aluminum foil pan on the other side and fill halfway with water. Sprinkle a handful of drained chips over the coals. **IN A GAS GRILL,** preheat on High. Turn one burner off, and adjust the other burner(s) to Medium. Place a large disposable aluminum foil pan on the Off burner and fill halfway with water. Place a handful of drained chips in the metal chip box. Or, wrap a handful of chips in aluminum foil, pierce a few holes in the foil, and place on the heat source.

4. Remove the pork roast from the marinade. The butter will have solidified, but leave any clinging bits on the roast. Place the roast over the pan and cover the grill. Cook, basting occasionally with the remaining marinade, until an instant-read thermometer inserted in the center of the roast registers 155° F, about 1½ hours. Add additional ignited coals and chips as needed to maintain a grill temperature of about 350° F. **IN A GAS GRILL,** add more chips or foil packets every 30 minutes. (If your grill doesn't have a thermostat on its lid, place an oven thermometer next to the roast to get a reading.)

5. Transfer the roast to a serving platter and let stand for 10 minutes before carving.

Flashover Pork Tenderloin

Makes 6 to 8 servings

A flashover strikes fear into firefighters. When a fire's heat has built up to a certain point, everything in the room, including unburned gases, can instantly ignite (or "flash"), exploding into a deadly ball of flame. The peppercorns in this recipe, although benign, are hot enough to dub this pork tenderloin "flashover."

> Two 12-ounce pork tenderloins
> ¼ cup Worcestershire sauce
> 2 tablespoons Dijon mustard
> 1 tablespoon vegetable oil
> 2 teaspoons cracked black peppercorns (crushed in a mortar or under a
>   heavy skillet)

1. Rinse the tenderloins and pat dry with paper towel. Fold the thin end of each tenderloin back so the tenderloin is the same thickness throughout its length and tie with kitchen twine.

2. In a small bowl, whisk together the Worcestershire sauce, mustard, oil, and cracked peppercorns. Place the tenderloins and marinade in a zippered plastic bag. Close the bag and refrigerate for at least 1 hour, and up to 2 hours.

3. Build a charcoal fire in an outdoor grill and let burn until covered with white ash. **FOR A GAS GRILL,** preheat on High. Turn one burner off, leaving the other burner(s) on High.

4. Lightly oil the cooking grate. Place the tenderloins over the coals and cover. Grill, turning occasionally, until seared on all sides, about 6 minutes. Move to the cooler, outer perimeter of the grill, not directly over the coals. **FOR A GAS GRILL,** cook the tenderloins over the High burner until browned, about 6 minutes. Transfer to the Off burner and cover.

5. Cook for 8 to 12 minutes, until an instant-read thermometer inserted in the centers of the tenderloins reads 155° F.

6. Transfer to a cutting board and let stand for 5 minutes. Slice the tenderloins, holding the knife at a slight angle. Serve immediately.

Grandma Vanasco's Apple-and-Cheddar-Stuffed Pork Chops

FIREFIGHTER THOMAS VANASCO ▪ ENGINE COMPANY 299 ▪ NEW YORK FIRE DEPARTMENT ▪ NEW YORK, NEW YORK

Makes 4 servings

Tom says he got his best recipes from his Grandma Vanasco. With just a few ingredients, you can have these stuffed pork chops ready for the grill in no time.

> Four 12-ounce center-cut pork chops, cut about 1 inch thick
> 1 Golden Delicious apple, peeled, cored, and cut into 12 slices
> ½ cup shredded sharp Cheddar cheese
> 2 teaspoons vegetable oil
> ½ teaspoon salt
> ¼ teaspoon freshly ground black pepper

1. Using a sharp knife, cut a deep pocket into the center of each pork chop. Stuff each pocket with 3 apple slices and 2 tablespoons cheese. Brush the chops with the oil and season with the salt and pepper.

2. Build a charcoal fire in an outdoor grill and let burn until covered with white ash. **IN A GAS GRILL,** preheat on High.

3. Leave the coals heaped in a mound in the center of the grill. Do not spread them out. Lightly oil the cooking grate. Place the chops over the coals and cover. Grill, turning once, until seared on both sides, about 5 minutes. Move the chops to the cooler, outside perimeter of the grill, not directly over the coals. **IN A GAS GRILL,** grill on High until seared on both sides, about 5 minutes, then adjust the heat to Medium.

4. Cover and cook until an instant-read thermometer inserted in the center of a pork chop reads 155° F, 10 to 15 minutes. Serve immediately.

Smoked Pork Chops with Grilled Peaches

DONNA NICOLOSI ▪ LONG ISLAND, NEW YORK

Makes 4 servings

Donna is my sister, an excellent cook, and wife to Suffolk County Police Officer Mike Nicolosi. Now I have a nephew, Nicholas, and between his mother and me, I'm sure he'll learn his way around the kitchen. This is one of the best grill recipes around—smoke-grilled at a low temperature to ensure the deepest smoky flavor.

1 tablespoon sugar
1 teaspoon salt
$\frac{1}{2}$ teaspoon freshly ground black pepper
Four 12-ounce center-cut pork chops, cut about 1 inch thick
3 ripe medium peaches
1 tablespoon fresh lemon juice
3 cups hickory wood chips, soaked in water for 30 minutes and drained
1 tablespoon unsalted butter, melted

1. In a small bowl, combine the sugar, salt, and pepper. Season the chops with the mixture. Cover and refrigerate for 2 hours.

2. Meanwhile, to prepare the peaches, bring a medium saucepan of water to a boil over high heat. Boil the peaches just until the skins loosen, 30 to 60 seconds. Using a slotted spoon, transfer the peaches to a bowl of cold water. Remove the skins and cut each peach into 6 wedges. Place in a bowl, toss with the lemon juice, cover, and set aside.

3. Build a charcoal fire (use about 3 pounds of briquettes) on one side of an outdoor grill and let burn until covered with white ash. Place a large disposable aluminum foil pan on the empty side of the grill and fill halfway with water. Sprinkle the drained chips over the coals. **IN A GAS GRILL,** preheat on High. Turn one burner off, and adjust the other burner(s) to Medium. Place a large disposable aluminum foil pan over the Off burner and fill halfway with water. Place the drained chips in the metal chip box. Or, wrap the chips in aluminum foil, pierce a few holes in the foil, and place on the heat source.

4. Lightly oil the cooking grate. Place the chops over the pan and cover. Cook, adding more ignited coals and chips as needed to maintain a temperature of about 300° F, until an instant-read thermometer inserted in the center of a chop reads 155° F, about $1^{1}/_{4}$ hours. **IN A GAS GRILL,** add more chips or foil packets every 30 minutes. (If your grill doesn't have a thermostat on its lid, place an oven thermometer next to the chops to get a reading.) Transfer the chops to a serving platter and cover with aluminum foil to keep warm.

5. Brush the cooking grate clean and lightly oil. Brush the peaches with the butter. Place over the coals and cover. **IN A GAS GRILL,** increase the heat to High. Don't add any more wood chips. Grill the peaches, turning once, just until heated through, about 5 minutes. Serve the peaches with the pork chops.

Two-Jamaicas Jerked Pork Chops with Mango Salsa

FIREFIGHTER THOMAS PELLEGRINO ▪ ENGINE COMPANY 142 ▪ NEW YORK FIRE DEPARTMENT ▪ NEW YORK, NEW YORK

Makes 4 servings

Tom and I entered fire service together and still keep in touch. There are two Jamaicas—the one in the Caribbean, and the neighborhood where Tom is a firefighter in Queens, New York. "Jerked" pork chops are soaked in a special sauce (allspice, lime juice, and Scotch bonnet chiles are just a few of the exotic ingredients), then grilled over smoky coals. This is barbecue, Jamaican-style.

> **Four 12-ounce center-cut pork chops, cut about 1-inch thick**
> **Jamaican Jerk Marinade (page 62)**
> **Mango-Jalapeño Salsa (page 30)**

1. In a zippered plastic bag, combine the pork chops and marinade. Close the bag and refrigerate for at least 2 hours, and up to 4 hours. Remove from the refrigerator 30 minutes before grilling.

2. Build a charcoal fire in an outdoor grill and let burn until the coals are covered with white ash. **IN A GAS GRILL,** preheat on High.

3. Remove the pork chops from the marinade. Place on the grill and cover. Grill, turning occasionally, until the chops show no sign of pink when pierced at a bone, 10 to 12 minutes. If the fire flares up, move the chops to the cooler perimeter of the grill, not directly over the coals, and cover. (Or turn one gas burner off and move the chops over to the Off burner and cover.) Serve hot, with the mango salsa.

Grilled Sausage and Vegetable Kebabs

FIREFIGHTER TOM DAVOLI ▪ ENGINE COMPANY ▪ SPOFFORD FIRE DEPARTMENT ▪ SPOFFORD, NEW HAMPSHIRE

Makes 6 servings

These pizza-flavored kebabs can be made with either pork or turkey Italian sausage. Tom precooks the sausage to remove some of the fat that can cause flare-ups.

> 1 pound (6 links) hot or sweet Italian sausage
> $\frac{1}{2}$ cup bottled pizza sauce
> 1 teaspoon dried basil
> 6 long bamboo skewers, soaked in water for 30 minutes and drained
> 1 large zucchini, cut into 12 pieces
> 1 medium red bell pepper, seeded and cut into 12 squares

1. Prick each sausage link a few times with a fork. Place in a large skillet and add enough cold water to cover. Bring to a boil over medium heat. Simmer for 5 minutes. Drain and cool completely. Cut the sausage into $1\frac{1}{2}$-inch pieces.

2. In a small bowl, mix the pizza sauce and basil. Set aside.

3. Build a charcoal fire in an outdoor grill and let burn until covered with white ash. **IN A GAS GRILL,** preheat on High.

4. Lightly oil the cooking grate. On each skewer, alternate the sausage, zucchini, and red pepper pieces. Place on the grill and cover. Grill, turning occasionally, until the sausage is cooked through, about 15 minutes. During the last 8 minutes, brush frequently with the pizza sauce. Serve hot.

Veal Chops Oregano

Makes 4 servings

Veal chops can be grilled, but they need to be well-basted with olive oil to keep them from drying out. Oregano adds punch to the mild-flavored veal.

Eight 5-ounce veal loin chops, cut about $\frac{1}{2}$ inch thick
1 tablespoon olive oil
$1\frac{1}{2}$ teaspoons dried oregano
$\frac{3}{4}$ teaspoon salt
$\frac{1}{4}$ teaspoon freshly ground black pepper
Lemon wedges

1. Brush the veal chops with the oil, and season with the oregano, salt, and pepper. Cover and refrigerate for at least 1 hour, and up to 4 hours. Remove from the refrigerator 30 minutes before grilling.

2. Build a hot charcoal fire in an outdoor grill and let the coals burn until covered with white ash. Protecting your hands with an oven mitt, use a long garden trowel or some other utensil to bank the coals into a steep slope. **IN A GAS GRILL,** preheat on High.

3. Place the chops over the higher, hotter area of the sloped coals. Grill until both sides are seared, turning once, about 5 minutes. Move the chops over to the lower, cooler area of the coals and cover the grill. **IN A GAS GRILL,** grill the chops, turning once, until seared on both sides, about 5 minutes. Reduce the heat to Medium.

4. Cook, turning occasionally, until the chops feel firm when pressed in the center, 3 to 5 minutes. Serve immediately, with the lemon wedges for squeezing over the chops.

Chicken and Turkey

Classic BBQ Chicken

Makes 6 to 8 servings

I've seen barbecued chicken treated pretty poorly by backyard cooks. They think they're doing a good thing by marinating the chicken first in thick red barbecue sauce, but by the time the chicken is cooked through, the sauce is burned black. Even worse, to my mind, is the habit of partially cooking the chicken before grilling, which adds no flavor to the end result, and makes it hard to gauge doneness.

My way will be new to most cooks, but believe me, it works. The chicken is cooked by the indirect method, so the fat can cook out of the skin, yet not drip onto the coals and cause flare-ups. A little lemon-and-oil marinade is really unnecessary, but I know that most people can't imagine barbecued chicken without a marinade, so I do it to make them happy. Don't brush your sauce onto the chicken until the last 10 minutes, or you'll have blackened chicken—and that isn't so delicious.

If you wish, sprinkle the coals with soaked, drained wood chips (or add the chips to your gas grill's metal chip holder).

> Two 4-pound chickens, cut into 8 pieces each
> $\frac{1}{4}$ cup fresh lemon juice
> $\frac{1}{4}$ cup olive oil
> 2 garlic cloves, crushed through a press
> 1 teaspoon salt
> $\frac{1}{2}$ teaspoon freshly ground black pepper
> $1\frac{1}{2}$ cups tomato-based barbecue sauce, such as Cup-of-Joe BBQ Sauce (page 75)

I. Rinse the chicken and pat dry with paper towels. In a small bowl, whisk together the lemon juice, oil, garlic, salt, and pepper. Divide the chicken and lemon marinade between 2 zippered plastic bags. Refrigerate for at least 1 hour, and up to 2 hours.

2. Build a charcoal fire in an outdoor grill and let burn until covered with white ash. Leave the coals heaped in a mound in the center of the grill. Do not spread out. **IN A GAS GRILL,** preheat on High. Turn one burner off, and adjust the other burner(s) to High.

3. Remove the chicken from the marinade. Lightly oil the cooking grate. Arrange the chicken around the cooler, outer perimeter of the grill, not directly over the coals, and cover. **IN A GAS GRILL,** place the chicken over the Off burner and cover.

4. Grill, turning occasionally, until the chicken shows no sign of pink when pierced at the bone, about 50 minutes. During the last 10 minutes, turn the chicken twice, brushing each time with a generous amount of sauce. Serve hot.

Red Devil Chicken

Makes 4 servings

Firefighters have a nickname (or a curse name) for fire, "The Red Devil." This chicken is so spicy with red pepper, Italians call it *pollo alla diavola,* or "chicken, devil-style." Split, splayed on the grill, and weighted under a foil-wrapped brick, the end result is a particularly juicy bird with a crispy skin. A heavy cast-iron skillet works well as a weight, also.

> One 4-pound chicken, rinsed and patted dry
> $\frac{1}{3}$ cup dry white wine
> $\frac{1}{3}$ cup olive oil
> 2 tablespoons fresh lemon juice
> 2 garlic cloves, crushed through a press
> 2 teaspoons dried oregano
> 1 teaspoon hot red pepper flakes
> $\frac{1}{2}$ teaspoon salt

1. Using a cleaver or heavy knife, cut down one side of the backbone to cut the chicken in half. Cut down the other side and discard the backbone. Place the chicken on a work surface, skin side up. Press hard on the breastbone with the heel of your hand to flatten the chicken.

2. In a small bowl, whisk together the wine, oil, lemon juice, garlic, oregano, red pepper flakes, and salt. Place the chicken and marinade in a zippered plastic bag. Close the bag and refrigerate for at least 1 hour, and up to 2 hours.

3. Build a charcoal fire in one side of an outdoor grill and let burn until covered with white ash. Place a large disposable aluminum foil pan on the empty side of the grill and fill halfway with water. **IN A GAS GRILL,** preheat on High. Turn one burner off, and keep the other burner(s) on High. Place the foil pan on the Off burner, and fill halfway with water.

4. Remove the chicken from the marinade. Lightly oil the cooking grate. Place, skin-side down, over the pan. Weight the chicken with an aluminum foil-wrapped brick. Cover and cook for 25 minutes. Remove the brick and turn the chicken. Cover and continue cooking (without the brick) until the chicken shows no sign of pink when pierced at the thighbone, about 25 minutes more.

5. Using a cleaver or heavy knife, chop the chicken into quarters, and serve hot.

Grilled Chicken with Dijon Mustard and Tarragon

**LT. TERENCE "SPIDER" WALSH ▪ ENGINE COMPANY 230 ▪
NEW YORK FIRE DEPARTMENT ▪ NEW YORK, NEW YORK**

Makes 6 to 8 servings

It's impossible for me to choose a favorite way to grill chicken, but this is definitely a contender for the Top Ten. You can experiment with flavored mustards to give the marinade a personal stamp. It comes from my friend Spider, who decided to hit the books and become a fire officer. He is also a pilot and a plane owner, and we spent many weekends flying to the Hamptons or Hunter Mountain, which are big hangouts for firefighters. (Of course this was before he got married!)

Two 4-pound chickens, cut into 8 pieces each
1 cup Dijon mustard
$\frac{1}{4}$ cup dry white wine
$\frac{1}{4}$ cup olive oil
2 scallions, white and green parts, finely chopped
2 teaspoons dried tarragon
$\frac{1}{4}$ teaspoon hot red pepper sauce, such as Tabasco

1. Rinse the chicken and pat dry with paper towels. In a medium bowl, whisk the mustard, wine, oil, scallions, tarragon, and hot pepper sauce. Divide the chicken and marinade between two zippered plastic bags. Close the bags and refrigerate for at least 1 hour, and up to 4 hours.

2. Build a charcoal fire in an outdoor grill and let burn until covered with white ash. Leave the coals heaped in a mound in the center of the grill. Do not spread them out. **IN A GAS GRILL,** preheat on High. Turn one burner off, and keep the other burner(s) on High.

3. Remove the chicken from the marinade. Lightly oil the cooking grate. Arrange the chicken around the cooler, outer perimeter of the grill, not directly over the coals, and cover. **IN A GAS GRILL,** place over the Off burner(s).

4. Grill, basting occasionally with the marinade, for 25 minutes. Turn the chicken, cover, and continue cooking until the chicken shows no sign of pink when pierced at the thigh bone, 20 to 25 minutes more. Do not baste during the last 10 minutes of cooking. Serve hot.

Grill-Roasted Whole Chicken with Garlic, Lemon, and Rosemary

CHIEF CURT VARONE ▪ PROVIDENCE FIRE DEPARTMENT ▪ PROVIDENCE, RHODE ISLAND

Makes 4 servings

I have done many health and fitness seminars for Chief Varone, another chief who does his best to be sure his firefighters are as fit as they can be. I have gotten many thanks from the firefighters who've attended our seminars, and many great recipes, too. Here's a recipe from the Chief—rubbed inside and out with a garlicky rosemary oil, the fragrant chicken tastes as wonderful as it looks.

One 4-pound whole chicken
1 lemon
2 tablespoons olive oil, preferably extra-virgin
1½ tablespoons chopped fresh rosemary or 1½ teaspoons dried
2 tablespoons lemon juice
2 garlic cloves, crushed through a press
½ teaspoon salt
¼ teaspoon freshly ground black pepper

1. Rinse the chicken and pat dry. Slip your fingers under the skin to loosen it from the breast and thigh areas.

2. Squeeze the juice from the lemon, reserving the juiced lemon halves and 1 tablespoon juice. In a small bowl, combine the oil, rosemary, lemon juice, garlic, salt, and pepper. Rub the oil mixture underneath the skin, inside the chicken, and all over the chicken skin. Place the lemon halves and tablespoon lemon juice in the chicken cavity. Cover loosely with plastic wrap and let stand at room temperature for 30 minutes.

3. Build a charcoal fire in one side of an outdoor grill and let burn until covered with white ash. Place a large disposable aluminum foil pan in the empty area of the grill and fill halfway with water. **FOR A GAS GRILL,** preheat on High. Turn one burner off, and keep the other burner(s) on High. Place a large disposable aluminum foil pan on the Off burner(s) and fill halfway with water.

4. Lightly oil the cooking grate. Place the chicken over the pan and cover. Cook until the meat shows no sign of pink when pierced at the thigh, about $1^3/_4$ hours. After 45 minutes, add more ignited coals to the charcoal grill.

5. Transfer to a serving platter and let stand for 10 minutes before carving.

Classic Grilled Chicken Breasts

Makes 4 servings

Night after night, millions of Americans turn to boneless, skinless chicken breasts to make a fast meal. The problem is, most of the time, they cook the breasts so fast they turn tough as shoe leather, especially on the grill.

This dilemma is easy to solve. There is a lot of fat in poultry skin, and it naturally bastes the breast during cooking. When the skin is removed, the breast can dry out. So the first solution is a marinade or glaze. But even more important is the heat level. Don't incinerate the chicken breast over high heat. Sear the breast over hot coals, then move to the cooler edges of the grill to finish cooking. If you have a gas grill, medium heat throughout is the way to go.

> **Four 6- to 7-ounce boneless, skinless chicken breasts, pounded slightly to even thickness**
> **White Wine and Herb Marinade (page 58)**

1. Place the chicken breasts and marinade in a zippered plastic bag. Refrigerate for at least 1 hour, and up to 4 hours.

2. Build a charcoal fire in an outdoor grill and let burn until covered with white ash. Leave the coals heaped in a mound in the center of the grill. Do not spread out. **IN A GAS GRILL,** preheat on High, then adjust to Medium.

3. Lightly oil the cooking grate. Remove the chicken from the marinade, but do not pat dry. Place directly over the coals and cover. Grill, turning once, until seared on both sides, about 5 minutes. Transfer to the cooler, outside perimeter of the grill, not directly over the coals. Cover and cook until the chicken breasts feel firm when pressed in the centers, 5 to 10 minutes. **IN A GAS GRILL,** cook over Medium heat throughout. Serve hot.

Basil-Marinated Chicken Breasts

Makes 6 servings

In my neck of the woods, everyone's summer garden is packed with basil leaves. This green marinade is one of the best ways to enjoy a bumper crop. Boneless, skinless breasts should be well-marinated to keep them from drying out.

MARINADE

$1^1/_2$ cups packed fresh basil leaves
2 garlic cloves, crushed with a knife
$^1/_3$ cup dry white wine
3 tablespoons olive oil
3 tablespoons Dijon mustard
$^1/_2$ teaspoon salt
$^1/_4$ teaspoon hot red pepper flakes
Six 6- to 7-ounce boneless, skinless chicken breasts, pounded slightly
   to even thickness

1. To make the marinade, combine the basil, garlic, wine, oil, mustard, salt, and red pepper in a food processor fitted with a metal blade and process until smooth. (To make the marinade in a blender, use half the ingredients at one time and blend until smooth.)

2. Place the chicken breasts and marinade in a zippered plastic bag. Close the bag and refrigerate for at least 1 hour, and up to 4 hours.

3. Build a charcoal fire in an outdoor grill and let burn until covered with white ash. Do not spread out the coals, but leave them in a mound in the center. **IN A GAS GRILL,** preheat on High. Turn one burner off, and keep the other burner(s) on High.

4. Remove the chicken from the marinade, but do not wipe the clinging marinade off the chicken. Lightly oil the cooking grate. Place the chicken breasts on the cooler, outside perimeter of the grill, not directly over the coals, and cover. **IN A GAS GRILL,** place the chicken over the Off burner and cover.

5. Grill, turning occasionally, until the chicken feels firm when pressed in the thickest part, 20 to 25 minutes. Serve hot.

Chicken Breasts with
Cilantro Marinade and Tomatillo Salsa

**FIREFIGHTER BRIAN "BARNEY" PERICONE ▪ LINDEN FIRE DEPARTMENT ▪
LINDEN, NEW JERSEY**

Barney is quite a cook. When I saw the recipe, I thought a chef had sent it
to me instead of a firefighter because the ingredients were so sophisticated.
This is a dish for when you have special guests you want to impress with
your cooking. Barney likes to serve it with white rice mixed with cooked
black beans.

MARINADE

$\frac{1}{2}$ cup dry white wine, such as Chardonnay
$\frac{1}{4}$ cup fresh lime juice
$\frac{1}{4}$ cup chopped fresh cilantro
2 tablespoons finely chopped shallots
2 garlic cloves, minced
$\frac{1}{2}$ teaspoon salt
$\frac{1}{2}$ teaspoon coarsely ground black pepper
$\frac{1}{2}$ cup olive oil, preferably extra-virgin

Four 6- to 7-ounce boneless, skinless chicken breasts
Green and Red Salsa (page 28)

1. In a medium bowl, whisk together the wine, lime juice, cilantro, shallots,
garlic, salt, and pepper. Gradually whisk in the oil.

2. In a zippered plastic bag, combine the chicken breasts and marinade. Close
the bag and marinate for at least 2 hours, and up to 8 hours.

3. Build a charcoal fire in an outdoor grill and let burn until covered with
white ash. Do not spread out the coals, but leave them heaped in a mound in
the center of the grill. **IN A GAS GRILL,** preheat on High. Turn one burner off
and keep the other burner(s) on High.

4. Remove the chicken from the marinade, but do not pat dry. Lightly oil the cooking grate. Place directly over the coals and cover. Grill, turning once, until seared on both sides, about 5 minutes. Transfer to the cooler, outside perimeter of the grill, not directly over the coals, and cover. **IN A GAS GRILL,** cook the breasts over the High burner, turning once, until seared on both sides, about 5 minutes. Move to the Off burner and cover.

5. Cook until the chicken breasts feel firm when pressed in the centers, 5 to 10 minutes. Serve the chicken breasts hot, passing the salsa at the table.

Chicken Breasts with
Prosciutto, Asparagus, and Mozzarella

Makes 6 servings

As probably the most flavorful ham in the world, a little bit of prosciutto goes a long way. Usually it is sliced paper thin, but ask the person at the deli counter to slice it a hair thicker—this prosciutto isn't going to be served with melon, but with grilled chicken breasts topped with cheese and asparagus. If asparagus is out of season, substitute pieces of roasted red pepper.

$^1\!/_4$ cup dry Marsala
2 tablespoons olive oil
$^1\!/_2$ teaspoon salt
$^1\!/_4$ teaspoon freshly ground black pepper
Four 6- to 7-ounce boneless, skinless chicken breasts
24 asparagus spears, woody ends discarded
1 large slice prosciutto or Black Forest ham, cut into 6 pieces to
　　　fit chicken breasts
4 ounces mozzarella, thinly sliced

1. In a small bowl, whisk together the Marsala, oil, salt, and pepper. In a zippered plastic bag, combine the chicken breasts and marinade. Close the bag and refrigerate for at least 1 hour, and up to 4 hours.

2. Bring a large saucepan of lightly salted water to a boil over high heat. Add the asparagus and cook until just crisp-tender, about 3 minutes. Drain and rinse under cold running water. Pat dry with paper towels. Set the asparagus aside. If necessary, trim the asparagus to fit the breasts.

3. Build a charcoal fire in an outdoor grill and let burn until covered with white ash. Do not spread out the coals, but leave them heaped in a mound in the center of the grill. **IN A GAS GRILL,** preheat on High. Turn one burner off, and keep the other burner(s) on High.

4. Remove the chicken from the marinade, but do not pat dry. Lightly oil the cooking grate. Place the chicken breasts directly over the coals and cover. Grill, turning once, until seared on both sides, about 5 minutes. Transfer to the cooler, outside perimeter of the grill, not directly over the coals, and cover. **IN A GAS GRILL,** cook the chicken breasts over the High burner, turning once, until seared on both sides, about 5 minutes. Move to the Off burner and cover.

5. Cook until the chicken is almost cooked through, about 5 minutes. Using tongs, remove the breasts from the grill. Cover each breast with a piece of prosciutto, 4 asparagus spears, and sliced mozzarella. Return to the cool part of the grill. **IN A GAS GRILL,** place the breasts over the Off burner. Cover and cook until the cheese melts, 3 to 5 minutes. Serve immediately.

Grilled Chicken Salad with Bourbon-Mustard Dressing

FIREFIGHTER SCOTT PELTIN ▪ PHOENIX FIRE DEPARTMENT ▪ PHOENIX, ARIZONA

Makes 4 servings

Scott's recipe was the inspiration for this main-course warm chicken salad with a bourbon-spiked marinade that does double-duty as a dressing.

MARINADE/DRESSING

$\frac{1}{2}$ cup cider vinegar

3 tablespoons bourbon

2 tablespoons spicy brown mustard

1 tablespoon light brown sugar

2 garlic cloves, crushed through a press

$\frac{1}{2}$ teaspoon salt

$\frac{1}{2}$ teaspoon freshly ground black pepper

$\frac{1}{2}$ cup plus $\frac{1}{3}$ cup olive oil

Four 6- to 7-ounce boneless, skinless chicken breasts, slightly pounded to an even thickness

1 large head red leaf lettuce, rinsed, dried, and torn into bite-sized pieces

4 medium tomatoes, cut into $\frac{1}{2}$-inch dice

1 medium cucumber, peeled and sliced

2 medium carrots, shredded

6 radishes, shredded

1. To make the marinade/dressing, whisk together the vinegar, bourbon, mustard, brown sugar, garlic, salt, and pepper in a small bowl. Gradually whisk in $\frac{1}{2}$ cup of the olive oil. In a zippered plastic bag, combine the chicken breasts and $\frac{1}{2}$ cup of the marinade mixture. Close the bag and refrigerate for at least 1 hour, and up to 2 hours.

2. Whisk the remaining $\frac{1}{3}$ cup oil into the remaining marinade mixture to become the salad dressing. Cover and refrigerate until ready to use.

3. Build a charcoal fire in an outdoor grill and let burn until covered with white ash. **IN A GAS GRILL,** preheat on High. Turn one burner off, and keep the other burner(s) on High.

4. Remove the chicken from the marinade, but do not pat dry. Lightly oil the cooking grate. Place the chicken over the coals and cover. Grill, turning once, until seared on both sides, about 5 minutes. Transfer to the cooler, outer perimeter of the grill, not directly over the coals, and cover. **IN A GAS GRILL,** grill over the High burner, turning once, until seared on both sides, about 5 minutes. Move to the area above the Off burner and cover.

5. Cook until the chicken breasts feel firm when pressed in the centers, 5 to 10 minutes. Cool slightly, then cut the chicken into bite-sized pieces.

6. Arrange the lettuce, tomatoes, cucumber, carrots, and radishes on a large platter. Place the chicken on the vegetables and drizzle the dressing on top. Serve immediately.

Chicken Breasts Stuffed with Ricotta and Basil

Makes 6 servings

These stuffed breasts are great dinner party fare. Buy chicken breast halves with the skin and bone on, then use a sharp knife to bone the breasts, leaving each breast in one piece with the skin attached (or ask the butcher to bone them for you).

> Six 8-ounce boneless chicken breast halves, skin on
> 1 cup ricotta cheese
> 3 tablespoons freshly grated Parmesan cheese
> 2 tablespoons chopped fresh basil or $1\frac{1}{2}$ teaspoons dried
> 2 tablespoons dried breadcrumbs
> $\frac{1}{2}$ teaspoon salt
> $\frac{1}{4}$ teaspoon freshly ground black pepper

1. Rinse the chicken breasts and pat dry with paper towels. In a medium bowl, mix the ricotta and Parmesan cheeses, basil, and breadcrumbs. Slip your fingers under the skin of one breast. Stuff the breast with about $\frac{1}{3}$ cup of the stuffing. Repeat with the remaining breasts and stuffing. Season the breasts with the salt and pepper.

2. Build a charcoal fire in one side of an outdoor grill and let burn until covered with white ash. **IN A GAS GRILL,** preheat on High. Turn one burner off, and keep the other burner(s) on High.

3. Lightly oil the cooking grate. Place the chicken breasts, skin-sides up, over the empty side of the grill. **IN A GAS GRILL,** place the breasts over the Off burner. Cover and cook until an instant-read thermometer inserted in the centers of the breasts reads 170° F, about 30 minutes. Serve immediately.

Chicken Breast Packets with Orange Sauce

FIREFIGHTER WILLIAM LUCKENBILL ▪ FLORENCE FIRE DEPARTMENT ▪ FLORENCE, NEW JERSEY

Makes 4 servings

Wrapped in a foil packet with orange juice, bell peppers, and jalapeños, these chicken breasts make their own sauce. Bill suggests varying the liquid as you please—try pineapple juice or beer.

Four 6- to 7-ounce boneless, skinless chicken breasts
1 tablespoon vegetable oil
$\frac{1}{2}$ teaspoon salt
$\frac{1}{4}$ teaspoon freshly ground black pepper
2 small red bell peppers, seeded and cut into $\frac{1}{4}$-inch-thick rings
1 jalapeño pepper, cut into thin rounds (remove the seeds, if you wish)
2 garlic cloves, cut into thin slivers
1 teaspoon unsalted lemon-pepper seasoning
4 tablespoons ($\frac{1}{2}$ stick) unsalted butter
1 cup fresh orange juice

1. Build a charcoal fire in an outdoor grill and let burn until covered with white ash. **IN A GAS GRILL,** preheat on High, then adjust to Medium.

2. Lightly oil the cooking grate. Brush the chicken breasts with the oil, then season with the salt and pepper. Grill the chicken breasts just until seared with grill markings on each side, about 1 minute. Set the breasts aside.

3. Tear off four 15-inch-long pieces of aluminum foil. Place the foil strips vertically on the work surface. Fold up the edges slightly to contain the orange juice. Place a chicken breast on the bottom third of each foil strip. Divide the red pepper, jalapeño, and garlic evenly over the breasts. Top each with $\frac{1}{4}$ teaspoon lemon-pepper and 1 tablespoon butter, then pour $\frac{1}{4}$ cup orange juice over each breast. Fold the foil over to enclose each breast, then tightly fold the edges to seal.

4. Place the foil packets on the grill and cover. Cook until the chicken is cooked through, about 12 minutes (open a foil packet to check). Serve immediately.

Chicken Breasts with Mushrooms and Marsala

Makes 4 servings

The foil-packet method of cooking chicken breasts is a great way to be sure they turn out nice and juicy. Here's another recipe, this time with Marsala and mushrooms.

Four 6- to 7-ounce boneless, skinless chicken breasts
1 tablespoon olive oil
8 ounces mushrooms, thinly sliced
4 teaspoons chopped shallots or scallions (white part only)
1 teaspoon dried thyme
1 teaspoon salt
$\frac{1}{2}$ teaspoon freshly ground black pepper
$\frac{1}{2}$ cup dry Marsala
4 tablespoons ($\frac{1}{2}$ stick) unsalted butter

1. Build a charcoal fire in an outdoor grill and let burn until covered with white ash. **IN A GAS GRILL,** preheat on High, then adjust to Medium.

2. Brush the chicken breasts with the oil. Lightly oil the cooking grate. Grill the chicken breasts just until seared with grill markings on each side, about 1 minute. The idea is to just mark the breasts, not cook them. Set the breasts aside.

3. Tear off four 15-inch-long pieces of aluminum foil. Place the foil strips vertically on the work surface. Fold up the edges slightly to contain the wine that will be added later. Place a chicken breast on the bottom third of each foil strip. On each breast, place one-fourth of the mushrooms and 1 teaspoon shallots. Sprinkle each with $\frac{1}{4}$ teaspoon dried thyme, $\frac{1}{4}$ teaspoon salt, and $\frac{1}{8}$ teaspoon pepper. Top with 2 tablespoons Marsala and 1 tablespoon butter. Fold the foil over to enclose each breast, then tightly fold the edges to seal.

4. Place the foil packets on the grill and cover. Cook until the chicken is cooked through, about 12 minutes (open a foil packet to check). Serve immediately.

Tandoori Chicken Breasts

Makes 4 servings

A tandoori is a kind of clay oven used by Indian cooks that creates intense heat. Tandoori-cooked foods are usually marinated in a spicy yogurt sauce.

> **Four 11-ounce chicken breast halves, with skin and bone**
> **2 tablespoons fresh lemon juice**
> **$\frac{1}{4}$ teaspoon salt**
> **Tandoori Marinade (page 64)**

1. Rub the chicken breasts with the lemon juice and salt. Place in a zippered plastic bag and add the marinade. Close the bag and refrigerate for at least 4 hours, and up to 24 hours—the longer the better.

2. Build a charcoal fire in an outdoor grill and let burn until covered with white ash. Do not spread out the coals, but leave them heaped in a mound. **IN A GAS GRILL,** preheat on High. Turn one burner off, and keep the other burner(s) on High.

3. Remove the chicken breasts from the marinade. Lightly oil the cooking grate. Place the chicken breasts on the cooler, outside perimeter of the grill, not directly over the coals, and cover. **IN A GAS GRILL,** place over the Off burner and cover.

4. Cook, turning occasionally, until the breasts show no sign of pink when pierced at the bone, about 40 minutes. Serve hot.

Chicken Hero Sandwiches

**FIREFIGHTER KEVIN NERNEY ▪ ENGINE COMPANY 299 ▪
NEW YORK FIRE DEPARTMENT ▪ NEW YORK, NEW YORK**

Makes 4 servings

Another one of the FDNY's better cooks, Kevin and his son Joey were both on TV when "Good Day NY" taped the whole show from our quarters. Here is his recipe for chicken hero sandwiches, which make a filling lunch or a light supper.

MARINADE

3 tablespoons red wine vinegar
$\frac{1}{2}$ teaspoon dried oregano
2 garlic cloves, crushed through a press
$\frac{1}{2}$ teaspoon salt
$\frac{1}{4}$ teaspoon hot red pepper flakes
$\frac{1}{3}$ cup olive oil

Four 6- to 7-ounce boneless, skinless chicken breasts, lightly pounded to
    an even thickness
4 ounces mozzarella cheese, thinly sliced
$\frac{1}{3}$ cup mayonnaise
2 tablespoons finely chopped basil leaves
4 soft French or Italian rolls, split
2 medium tomatoes, thinly sliced
1 small red onion, thinly sliced

1. To make the marinade, whisk together the vinegar, oregano, garlic, salt, and red pepper in a small bowl. Gradually whisk in the oil. Place the chicken breasts in a zippered plastic bag and add the marinade. Close the bag and refrigerate for at least 1 hour, and up to 2 hours.

2. Build a charcoal fire in an outdoor grill and let burn until covered with white ash. **IN A GAS GRILL,** preheat on High. Turn one burner off, and keep the other burner(s) on High.

3. Remove the chicken from the marinade, but do not pat dry. Lightly oil the cooking grate. Place the chicken breasts over the coals and cover. Grill, turning once, until seared on both sides, about 5 minutes. Transfer to the cooler, outside perimeter of the grill, not directly over the coals, and cover. **IN A GAS GRILL,** grill over the High burner, turning once, until seared on both sides, about 5 minutes. Move to the Off burner and cover.

4. Cook until the chicken breasts feel firm when pressed in the centers, 5 to 10 minutes. Top each breast with sliced mozzarella, cover, and cook until the mozzarella is beginning to melt, about 1 minute.

5. In a small bowl, mix the mayonnaise and basil. Spread on the rolls. Fill sandwiches with the chicken breasts, tomatoes, and onion. Cut each sandwich in half and serve warm.

Chicken Saté with Peanut Sauce

Makes 4 to 6 servings

Just a few years ago, something like this would have been considered pretty exotic. Now you can get peanut-flavored salad dressing at the supermarket! Serve these chicken mini-kebabs (called *satés* in Southeast Asia) and their peanut sauce as an appetizer, or as a main course with the Napa Cabbage and Pineapple Slaw on page 34. Hoisin sauce and chili paste with garlic can be found at Asian grocery stores and many supermarkets.

$1\frac{1}{2}$ **pounds boneless, skinless chicken breasts, cut into 1-inch by 3-inch strips, lightly pounded to an even thickness**
Indonesian Curry Marinade (page 65)
36 bamboo skewers

PEANUT SAUCE

$\frac{1}{2}$ **cup smooth peanut butter**
$\frac{1}{3}$ **cup low-sodium canned chicken broth**
$\frac{1}{4}$ **cup hoisin sauce**
1 tablespoon soy sauce
$\frac{1}{4}$ **teaspoon chili paste with garlic, or more to taste**

1. In a zippered plastic bag, combine the chicken breast strips and marinade. Close the bag and refrigerate for at least 1 hour, and up to 4 hours. Soak the bamboo skewers in water for 30 minutes. Then drain.

2. To make the peanut sauce, whisk together all of the ingredients in a medium bowl until smooth. Let stand at room temperature until ready to serve, up to 1 hour. If the sauce thickens, thin with additional broth or water.

3. Build a charcoal fire in an outdoor grill and let burn until covered with white ash. **IN A GAS GRILL,** preheat on High.

4. Remove the chicken strips from the marinade and thread onto the skewers. Lightly oil the cooking grate. Grill the kebabs, turning once, until the chicken is cooked through, about 5 minutes. Serve immediately, with the peanut sauce.

Sichuan Chicken Wings

Makes 4 to 6 servings

Whether you serve them as a main course with rice, or as an appetizer with the beverage of your choice (most firefighters would choose an Asian beer), these fire-hot Chinese-style wings make great nibbling.

3 pounds chicken wings
$\frac{1}{3}$ cup soy sauce
$\frac{1}{3}$ cup American-style chili sauce
$\frac{1}{3}$ cup rice vinegar
2 tablespoons vegetable oil
2 tablespoons shredded fresh ginger (use the large holes on a box grater)
2 tablespoons light brown sugar
2 garlic cloves, crushed through a press
1 teaspoon hot red pepper flakes
$\frac{1}{2}$ teaspoon salt

1. Using a cleaver or heavy knife, chop the chicken wings between the bones into 3 pieces each. Discard the wing tips.

2. In a medium bowl, whisk together the soy sauce, chili sauce, vinegar, oil, ginger, brown sugar, garlic, hot pepper flakes, and salt. Place the wings and marinade in a zippered plastic bag. Seal the bag and refrigerate for at least 2 hours, and up to 4 hours.

3. Build a charcoal fire in an outdoor grill and let burn until covered with white ash. Do not spread out the coals, but leave them heaped in a mound in the center of the grill. **IN A GAS GRILL,** preheat on High. Turn one burner off, and keep the other burner(s) on High.

4. Remove the wings from the marinade. Lightly oil the cooking grate. Place the wings on the cooler, outside perimeter of the grill, not directly over the coals, and cover. **IN A GAS GRILL,** place the wings over the Off burner and cover.

5. Cook until the wings show no sign of pink when pierced at a bone, about 45 minutes. Serve the wings hot or at room temperature.

Thai Chicken Wings with Sweet Garlic Dip

Makes 4 to 6 servings

Southeast Asian seasonings have made their mark on the American palate, and there's no turning back. These grilled chicken wings are based on *gai yaang*, a dish found on most Thai restaurant menus. You'll find lemongrass and fish sauce at an Asian grocer (if your supermarket doesn't already stock them).

3 pounds chicken wings
Thai Lemongrass Marinade (page 68)

SWEET GARLIC DIP

$\frac{1}{2}$ cup sugar
$\frac{1}{2}$ cup rice vinegar
2 garlic cloves, thinly sliced
$\frac{1}{2}$ teaspoon Asian chili paste with garlic

1. Using a cleaver or heavy knife, chop the chicken wings between the bones into 3 pieces each. Discard the wing tips. In a zippered plastic bag, combine the wings and the marinade. Seal the bag and refrigerate for at least 2 hours, and up to 8 hours.

2. To make the dip, combine the sugar, vinegar, $\frac{1}{4}$ cup water, and garlic in a small saucepan. Bring to a boil over medium heat, stirring to dissolve the sugar. Stir in the chili paste and cool completely. Set the dip aside at room temperature.

3. Build a charcoal fire in an outdoor grill and let burn until covered with white ash. Do not spread out the coals, but leave them heaped in a mound in the center of the grill. **IN A GAS GRILL,** preheat on High. Turn one burner off, and keep the other burner(s) on High.

4. Remove the wings from the marinade. Lightly oil the cooking grate. Place the wings on the cooler, outside perimeter of the grill, not directly over the coals, and cover. **IN A GAS GRILL,** place the wings over the Off burner and cover.

5. Cook until the wings show no sign of pink when pierced at a bone, about 45 minutes. Serve the wings hot or at room temperature, with the dip.

Country Cornish Game Hens

STEPHEN CHOROMANSKI ▪ OGDENSBURG, NEW JERSEY

Makes 4 servings

These Cornish hens deliver old-fashioned flavor. Stephen uses a store-bought herb-and-spice seasoning mix, but you can delete the paprika and experiment with the Italian Herb Rub (page 69), High-Octane Cajun Dry Rub (page 71), or Lone Star Dry Rub (page 70).

> Four $1\frac{1}{2}$-pound Cornish hens
> 1 small onion, cut into quarters
> 4 garlic cloves, crushed under a knife
> 4 tablespoons ($\frac{1}{2}$ stick) unsalted butter, melted
> 1 teaspoon herb-and-spice seasoning, such as Mrs. Dash's
> $\frac{1}{2}$ teaspoon sweet Hungarian paprika
> $\frac{1}{2}$ teaspoon salt
> $\frac{1}{4}$ teaspoon freshly ground black pepper
> $1\frac{1}{2}$ cups dry white wine or water

1. Rinse the hens inside and out and pat them dry with paper towels. Place an onion quarter and a garlic clove in the body cavity of each hen. Arrange the hens in a large, deep, disposable aluminum foil roasting pan. Brush the hens with the melted butter. In a small bowl, combine the herb seasoning, paprika, salt, and pepper. Sprinkle the hens with the seasoning mixture. Pour the wine around the hens. Cover the pan tightly with aluminum foil.

2. Build a charcoal fire in an outdoor grill and let burn until covered with white ash. Protecting your hands with oven mitts and using a garden trowel or another fireproof tool, spread out the coals into two banks, one on each side of the grill. **IN A GAS GRILL,** preheat on High. Turn one burner off, and keep the other burner(s) on High.

3. Place the pan over the empty area of the grill and cover. **IN A GAS GRILL,** place over the Off burner and cover. Cook for 40 minutes and remove the foil. Add more ignited coals to the charcoal grill. Continue cooking until a meat thermometer inserted in the thickest part of the thigh, not touching a bone, reads 170° F, about 40 more minutes.

4. Transfer the hens to a serving platter. Skim the fat off the cooking juices and serve the juices with the hens.

Grilled Cornish Hens with Orange Marinade

Makes 2 to 4 servings

Oranges and Cornish hens have an affinity for each other. Thawed orange juice concentrate gives this marinade a deeper orange flavor than fresh orange juice. For the best-tasting glaze, use imported orange marmalade—it is less sweet than our domestic version. The glaze is quite rich, and you may find half a bird to be enough for one serving, although hearty appetites will be able to handle a whole hen.

2 Cornish hens
$\frac{1}{2}$ cup thawed orange juice concentrate
$\frac{1}{2}$ cup vegetable oil
$\frac{1}{4}$ cup soy sauce
2 tablespoons shredded fresh ginger (use the large holes of a box grater)
2 garlic cloves, finely chopped
$\frac{1}{2}$ teaspoon hot red pepper flakes
$\frac{1}{2}$ cup orange marmalade, preferably imported bitter orange
    marmalade
2 tablespoons Dijon mustard

1. Rinse the hens inside and out and pat dry with paper towels. Using a heavy knife or a cleaver, cut each hen down one side of the backbone, then cut through the breastbone to cut in half. (Or have the butcher split the hens for you.)

2. In a medium bowl, whisk together the orange juice concentrate, oil, soy sauce, ginger, garlic, and red pepper flakes. Place the hens and marinade in a large zippered plastic bag. Seal the bag and refrigerate for at least 1 hour, and up to 4 hours.

3. Build a charcoal fire in one side of an outdoor grill and let burn until covered with white ash. Do not spread out the coals, but leave them heaped in a mound in the center of the grill. **IN A GAS GRILL,** preheat on High. Turn one burner off, and keep the other burner(s) on High.

4. In a small bowl, mix the marmalade and mustard. Set aside. Remove the hens from the marinade, leaving any clinging bits of ginger and garlic on them. Lightly oil the cooking grate. Place the hens on the cooler, outer perimeter of the grate, not directly over the coals, and cover. **IN A GAS GRILL,** place over the Off burner, and cover.

5. Grill, turning occasionally, until the hens show no sign of pink when pierced at the bone, about 50 minutes. During the last 10 minutes, move the hens directly over the coals. **IN A GAS GRILL,** increase the heat to High. Baste generously with the marmalade mixture to glaze the hens and turn occasionally. Serve immediately.

Cajun Grilled Turkey Breast

**FIREFIGHTER MICHAEL COLEMAN ▪ ENGINE COMPANY 259 ▪
NEW YORK FIRE DEPARTMENT ▪ NEW YORK, NEW YORK**

Makes 4 to 6 servings

Mike and I go way back. He went to probationary firefighter school (a military-style training academy for firefighters) with my brother Michael and me, and later I did a tour of duty at his firehouse. Mike gave me this recipe for my first cookbook, *The Healthy Firehouse Cookbook*, but missed my deadline. I'm glad to get to use it here. Mike's a good cook, and leftovers from this smoky turkey breast make the best turkey sandwiches for a quick firehouse lunch.

> One 2½-pound turkey breast half, with skin and bone
> 2 tablespoons vegetable oil
> 2 tablespoons Rookie's Cajun Rub (page 71)
> 1 tablespoon Worcestershire sauce
> ½ teaspoon salt
> 3 cups hickory chips, soaked in water for 30 minutes and drained

1. Loosen the skin from the breast to form a pocket. In a small bowl, mix the oil, Cajun rub, Worcestershire sauce, and salt. Rub half of the mixture under the skin, and the remainder over the outside of the breast. Cover and let stand at room temperature for 1 hour.

2. Build a charcoal fire in an outdoor grill and let burn until covered with white ash. Protecting your hands with oven mitts and using a garden trowel or another fireproof tool, spread out the coals into two banks, one on each side of the grill. Place a disposable aluminum foil pan in the empty area of the grill, and fill halfway with water. Sprinkle the coals with a handful of drained chips. **IN A GAS GRILL,** preheat on High. Turn one burner off, and keep the other burner(s) on High. Place a disposable aluminum foil pan on the Off burner and fill halfway with water. Add a handful of drained chips to the metal chip holder. Or, wrap the drained chips in aluminum foil, pierce a few holes in the foil, and place the foil packet directly on the heat source.

3. Lightly oil the cooking grate. Place the turkey breast, skin-side down, over the pan and cover. Grill the turkey breast, occasionally turning the breast and adding more chips, until a meat thermometer inserted in the thickest part of the breast reads 170° F., about 1 hour.

4. Transfer the breast to a carving board and let stand for 10 minutes before slicing.

Turkey Breast Antipasti Roulade

Makes 5 to 8 servings

Rolled with roasted bell pepper, provolone, and prosciutto, this turkey breast is filled with antipasti flavors. The turkey breast needs to be butterflied, like a leg of lamb. If you wish, serve with a spoonful of Italian Green Herb Sauce (page 72).

One 2-pound boneless and skinless turkey breast
4 thin slices prosciutto
2 ounces thinly sliced provolone cheese
1 small red bell pepper, roasted (see page 27), peeled, and cut into
$\frac{1}{2}$-inch-wide strips
8 large basil leaves
1 garlic clove, finely chopped
1 tablespoon olive oil
$\frac{1}{4}$ teaspoon salt
$\frac{1}{4}$ teaspoon freshly ground black pepper
$1\frac{1}{2}$ cups dry white wine

1. Place the turkey breast, smooth side down, on a work surface. Using a sharp knife, cut a deep incision into the thickest part of the meat on one side, slicing at a 45° angle. Be careful not to cut to all the way through the meat. Open this flap to one side like a book. Make another cut on the other side, and fold out in the other direction. Pound gently to flatten evenly.

2. Arrange the prosciutto slices, overlapping slightly and trimming as needed, over the surface of the turkey. Top with overlapping slices of provolone, then the roast pepper strips, and the basil. Sprinkle with the garlic. Roll up the turkey breast and tie crosswise and lengthwise with kitchen string. Brush with the oil and season with the salt and pepper.

3. Build a charcoal fire in one side of an outdoor grill and let burn until covered with white ash. Place a disposable aluminum foil pan on the empty side of the grill, and pour 1 cup of the wine into the pan. **IN A GAS GRILL,** preheat on

High. Turn one burner off, and keep the other burner(s) on High. Place a disposable aluminum foil pan on the Off burner, and pour 1 cup of the wine into the pan.

4. Lightly oil the cooking grate. Place the turkey roulade over the pan. Cover and grill, basting occasionally with the remaining $\frac{1}{2}$ cup wine, until an instant-read thermometer inserted in the center of the roulade reads 170° F, about $1\frac{1}{4}$ hours.

5. Transfer the roulade to a serving platter and let stand for 5 minutes. Remove the string and cut the meat into $\frac{1}{2}$-inch-thick slices.

Turkey Kielbasa with Vidalia Onions and Apples

**FIREFIGHTER EDWARD MARTIN ▪ LADDER COMPANY 152 ▪
NEW YORK FIRE DEPARTMENT ▪ NEW YORK, NEW YORK**

Makes 4 servings

Ed is actually one of the best firefighter cooks I know, but he doesn't cook too often. (I guess thirty years of fielding culinary commentary from fellow firefighter/food critics can make one shy away from the stove.) Every once in a while, we get treated to one of his special dishes, like these grilled turkey sausage packets. Sweet-tasting Vidalia onions and apples go great with kielbasa, especially the low-fat turkey variety.

> 1 pound turkey kielbasa, cut into 4 lengths
> 2 large Vidalia onions, thinly sliced
> 2 Granny Smith apples, peeled, cored, and thinly sliced
> $^3/_4$ cup lager beer
> $^1/_4$ cup light brown sugar
> $^1/_4$ cup spicy brown mustard

1. Build a charcoal fire in an outdoor grill and let burn until covered with white ash. **IN A GAS GRILL,** preheat on High.

2. Prick each piece of kielbasa a few times with a fork. Tear off four 15-inch-long pieces of aluminum foil. Place the foil strips vertically on a work surface. Fold up the edges slightly to contain the beer that will be added later. Place one-fourth of the onions and apples on the bottom third of each foil strip. Spoon 3 tablespoons beer, 1 tablespoon brown sugar, and 1 tablespoon mustard onto each portion, then top with a piece of kielbasa. Fold the foil over to enclose the ingredients, then tightly fold the edges to seal.

4. Place the foil packets on the grill and cover. Cook until the onions are tender (open a packet to check), 20 to 25 minutes. Serve immediately.

Curried Chicken Cheese Burgers

Makes 4 servings

When a plain burger just won't make it, grill up this spiced chicken version.
The combination of chutney, cheddar, and curry is exotic, and delicious.

> $1^1/_4$ **pounds ground chicken**
> **1 scallion, white and green parts, finely chopped**
> **2 tablespoons dried breadcrumbs**
> **2 teaspoons Madras-style curry powder**
> $^3/_4$ **teaspoon salt**
> **4 ounces sharp cheddar cheese, thinly sliced**
> **4 hamburger buns, toasted on the grill**
> **Thinly sliced cucumbers**
> **Mango chutney**

1. In a medium bowl, lightly mix the ground chicken, scallion, breadcrumbs, curry, and salt. Using wet hands, form into 4 burgers, each about 4 inches in diameter.

2. Build a charcoal fire in an outdoor grill and let burn down to medium heat. You should be able to hold your hand at grate level for 3 seconds. **IN A GAS GRILL,** preheat on High, then adjust to Medium.

3. Lightly oil the cooking grate. Place the burgers on the grill and cover. Grill, turning once, until the burgers are cooked through and spring back when pressed in the centers, 12 to 15 minutes. During the last 2 minutes, divide the cheese evenly over the tops of the burgers so it will melt.

4. Place the burgers in the buns and serve, topping each with cucumber slices and a dollop of chutney.

Classic BBQ Poultry Burgers

Makes 4 burgers

More and more cooks are making their burgers with ground turkey or chicken, making them as common as beef burgers at many cookouts. Poultry burgers can be great, if you follow a few guidelines.

Ground turkey can be made from white and dark meat combined (about 7 percent fat) or from all-white breast meat (about 1 percent fat). The all-breast meat, while very low in fat, makes a very dry burger, so I don't recommend it. Ground chicken has a higher fat content (about 10 percent) and is moister than either kind of ground turkey.

Turkey or chicken burgers should always be served cooked through, never rare. But that doesn't mean dried out like a hockey puck! Adding moistening ingredients to the ground poultry helps—Dijon mustard, chutney, plum sauce, teriyaki sauce, pizza sauce, salsa, or olive oil are just a few suggestions. Also, binders like dried breadcrumbs help hold in moisture. You can add up to 2 tablespoons each of a moistening ingredient or binder per $1\frac{1}{4}$ pounds of ground turkey, using a bit less for the moister ground chicken. (At my supermarket, ground poultry comes in $1\frac{1}{4}$-pound packages and makes four good-sized burgers.)

Just as high heat dries out boneless, skinless chicken breasts, a hot, hot grill is the poultry burger's enemy. Let the coals burn down to medium-hot, or cook them over Medium heat on a gas grill. Cook the burgers just until they feel firm when pressed in the center—that means they're well done.

1¼ pounds ground turkey or chicken

½ cup tomato-based barbecue sauce, such as Classic BBQ Sauce
(page 74)

2 tablespoons dried bread crumbs (optional, if using ground chicken)

1 teaspoon salt

¼ teaspoon freshly ground black pepper

4 hamburger buns, toasted on the grill

Sliced red onion, hamburger relish, lettuce leaves, and sliced tomatoes

1. Build a charcoal fire in an outdoor grill and let burn until the fire is medium-hot. You should be able to hold your hand at grate level for 3 seconds. **IN A GAS GRILL,** preheat on High, then reduce the heat to Medium.

2. In a medium bowl, combine the ground poultry, 2 tablespoons of the sauce, breadcrumbs if using, salt, and pepper. Using wet hands, lightly form into 4 burgers about 4 inches in diameter.

3. Lightly oil the cooking grate. Place the burgers on the grill and cover. Grill, turning once, until the burgers are cooked through and spring back when pressed in the center, 12 to 15 minutes. Brush with the sauce, turn, and grill for 30 seconds. Brush and turn again, and grill for 30 seconds more.

4. Place the burgers in the buns and let everyone chose their own fixings.

Turkey Pesto Burgers

Makes 4 servings

Basil, Parmesan cheese, and garlic combine to give these burgers the pesto treatment. Instead of hamburger buns, you could use squares of focaccia from an Italian bakery.

1¼ pounds ground turkey
¼ cup freshly grated Parmesan cheese
¼ cup finely chopped basil leaves
1 tablespoon olive oil
1 garlic clove, crushed through a press
½ teaspoon salt
¼ teaspoon freshly ground black pepper
4 hamburger buns, toasted on the grill
Sliced tomatoes

1. In a medium bowl, lightly mix the ground turkey, Parmesan cheese, basil, oil, garlic, salt, and pepper. Using wet hands, form into 4 burgers, each about 4 inches in diameter.

2. Build a charcoal fire in an outdoor grill and let burn down to medium heat. You should be able to hold your hand at grate level for 3 seconds. **IN A GAS GRILL,** preheat on High, then reduce the heat to Medium.

3. Lightly oil the cooking grate. Place the burgers on the grill and cover. Grill, turning once, until the burgers are cooked through and spring back when pressed in the centers, 12 to 15 minutes.

4. Place the burgers and tomatoes in the buns and serve.

Desserts and Drinks

Grilled Figs with Ricotta Cheese

Makes 4 servings

If you've never tried grilled figs, you're in for a treat. Try to make this with freshly prepared ricotta cheese from an Italian delicatessen, though a whole-milk supermarket variety will do fine.

> 12 ripe figs, halved lengthwise
> 3 tablespoons unsalted butter, melted
> 1 pound ricotta cheese
> $\frac{1}{2}$ cup honey

1. Build a charcoal fire in an outdoor grill and let the fire burn down to medium-hot. You should be able to hold your hand at grate level for 3 seconds. **IN A GAS GRILL,** preheat on High, then adjust to Medium.

2. Lightly oil the cooking grate. Grill the figs, turning occasionally and basting with the melted butter, until heated through, about 5 minutes.

3. Spoon the ricotta into 4 dessert bowls. Top each serving with one-fourth of the grilled figs, then drizzle with about 2 tablespoons honey. Serve immediately.

Mexican Bananas Foster

Makes 6 servings

These are fun to make and everyone goes crazy over them. If you are serving them to kids, substitute apple juice for the Kahlúa.

$^3/_4$ **cup packed light brown sugar**
$^3/_4$ **cup Kahlúa or other coffee-flavored liqueur**
12 tablespoons (1$^1/_2$ sticks) unsalted butter, cut into tablespoons
6 ripe bananas, peeled and cut into $^1/_2$-inch-thick rounds
Ground cinnamon, to taste
Vanilla ice cream

1. Build a charcoal fire in an outdoor grill and let burn until the coals are covered with white ash. Let the fire burn down to medium-hot (you should be able to hold your hand at grate level for 3 seconds). **IN A GAS GRILL,** preheat to Medium.

2. Tear off six 12-inch squares of aluminum foil. Fold one foil square in half. On the bottom half, place 2 tablespoons brown sugar, 2 tablespoons Kahlúa, 2 tablespoons butter, and 1 banana. Sprinkle with a pinch of cinnamon. Fold the foil over to form a packet, crimping the open edges to seal. Repeat with the remaining ingredients. (The packets can be prepared up to 1 hour ahead and kept at room temperature.)

3. Grill the packets until the sugar, Kahlúa, and butter are boiling (open a packet to check), 5 to 7 minutes. Open the packets, pour over bowls of ice cream, and serve immediately.

Grilled Pineapple Sundaes with Brandied Honey Sauce

Makes 6 servings

Topped with a sweet sauce, grilled pineapple slices can be part of a sensational sundae.

$\frac{1}{3}$ cup honey
$\frac{1}{3}$ cup brandy or Cognac
3 tablespoons unsalted butter, plus 1 tablespoon, melted
6 fresh pineapple slices, cut about $\frac{1}{2}$ inch thick, core removed
Vanilla ice cream
$\frac{1}{3}$ cup chopped unsalted macadamia nuts or cashews

1. Build a charcoal fire in an outdoor grill and let the fire burn down to medium-hot. You should be able to hold your hand at grate level for 3 seconds. **IN A GAS GRILL,** preheat on High, then adjust to Medium.

2. In a small saucepan, combine the honey, brandy, and 3 tablespoons butter. Place on the grill and bring to simmer. Remove from the heat.

3. Lightly oil the cooking grate. Brush the pineapple slices with the melted butter. Grill the pineapple slices, turning and basting occasionally with the sauce, until lightly glazed and heated through, about 5 minutes. Transfer to a cutting board and chop coarsely.

4. To serve, spoon the ice cream into individual bowls. Top with the pineapple, drizzle with the remaining sauce, and sprinkle with the nuts. Serve immediately.

Peach-Buttermilk Ice Cream

Makes about 1½ quarts

The new wave of ice cream makers has eliminated much of the mess associated with the old clunkers that needed rock salt and crushed ice. It's safe to say that everyone loves homemade peach ice cream, but tangy buttermilk makes this version not only delicious, but different as well.

6 ripe medium peaches (2 pounds)
½ cup granulated sugar
½ cup packed light brown sugar
1 tablespoon fresh lemon juice
1 teaspoon vanilla extract
¼ teaspoon almond extract
2 cups buttermilk

1. Bring a large pot of water to a boil over high heat. Add the peaches and cook just until the skins loosen, about 1 minute. (If the skins are stubborn, the peaches aren't as ripe as you thought; remove them and pare off the skin with a sharp knife.) Using a slotted spoon, transfer to a large bowl of iced water and let stand until cool enough to handle. Discard the skin and pits and coarsely chop the peaches. Transfer to a food processor.

2. Add the granulated sugar, brown sugar, lemon juice, vanilla, and almond extract to the food processor and puree. Transfer to a large bowl. Stir in the buttermilk. Cover and refrigerate until well chilled, about 2 hours.

3. Transfer to the container of an ice cream machine and process according to the manufacturer's directions.

4. Pack the ice cream into an airtight container, cover, and freeze for at least 2 hours to allow the ice cream to ripen and harden before serving.

Cantaloupe-Lime Granita

Makes I quart

Like so many fruit desserts, this one isn't worth making unless you have a good ripe specimen. In my neck of the woods, farmstands are loaded with juicy cantaloupes. If you suspect that your melon isn't ready, let it sit out at room temperature for a day or two to ripen. It should smell, well, like a melon, and yield slightly when pressed at the round end (not the stem end).

> 1 large ($3^3/_4$-pound) ripe cantaloupe
> $^3/_4$ cup sugar
> Grated zest of 1 lime
> 3 tablespoons fresh lime juice

I. Place a 9-inch by 13-inch metal baking dish in the freezer while preparing the cantaloupe mixture.

2. Using a sharp knife, cut away the cantaloupe peel. Scoop out the seeds. Cut the cantaloupe into 1-inch cubes. In a food processor fitted with a metal blade, puree the cantaloupe. Measure the puree: You should have 3 cups. Return the puree to the food processor, add the sugar, lime zest, and juice and pulse to combine.

3. Pour into the chilled pan. Freeze until the mixture freezes around the edges, about 1 hour, depending on your freezer's temperature. Using a large metal spoon, mix the frozen edges into the center (leave the spoon in the pan). Freeze, repeating the stirring procedure about every 30 minutes, until the mixture has frozen to a slushy consistency, 2 to 3 hours total freezing time. Serve immediately, scooped into chilled glasses. (The granita can be prepared up to 2 days ahead, transferred to a covered container, and stored in the freezer.)

Espresso Granita

Makes about 1 quart

Americans have (finally) learned to appreciate a good, bracing cup of espresso, and, it follows, coffee-flavored desserts like this icy coffee granita. Although there are home espresso machines, it's impractical to make 4 cups of espresso cup-by-cup. Just brew a pot of strong Italian roast coffee in your drip coffee maker, and you're on your way to a very cool dessert.

> $^{1}/_{2}$ cup finely ground Italian or French roast (espresso) beans
> $^{3}/_{4}$ cup sugar

1. Place a 9-inch by 13-inch metal baking dish in the freezer while preparing the coffee mixture.

2. Brew 4 cups of strong coffee, using $4^{1}/_{3}$ cups boiling water and the ground coffee. (I use a coffeemaker with a paper filter. If you use an electric coffeemaker, pour $4^{1}/_{3}$ cups cold water through the machine.) Add the sugar and stir to dissolve the sugar completely. Let stand until cool.

3. Pour into the chilled pan. Freeze until the mixture freezes around the edges, about 1 hour, depending on your freezer's temperature. Using a large metal spoon, mix the frozen edges into the center (leave the spoon in the pan). Freeze, repeating the stirring procedure about every 30 minutes, until the mixture has frozen to a slushy consistency, 2 to 3 hours total freezing time. Serve immediately, scooped into chilled glasses. (The granita can be prepared up to 2 days ahead, transferred to a covered container, and stored in the freezer.)

Vickie's Cantaloupe Soup with Papaya and Blueberries

FIREFIGHTER VICKIE WOLF ▪ REDDING FIRE DEPARTMENT ▪ REDDING, CALIFORNIA

Makes 4 to 6 servings

Colorful, refreshing, light—this chilled fruit soup has a lot going for it. Vickie prefers to serve the papaya-blueberry mixture on the side, so the fruits retain their individual textures and flavors. You could serve this for a first course, too.

2 ripe cantaloupes, skin and seeds removed, cut into chunks
$\frac{1}{4}$ cup fresh lime juice
2 tablespoons honey
1 ripe papaya, skin and seeds removed, cut into $\frac{1}{2}$-inch cubes
1 cup blueberries
1 tablespoon fresh lemon juice
$\frac{1}{2}$ cup chilled club soda
2 tablespoons finely chopped fresh mint

1. In a food processor or blender, puree the cantaloupe with the lime juice and honey. Transfer to a large bowl and cover.

2. In a medium bowl, mix the papaya, blueberries, and lemon juice and cover. Separately refrigerate the bowls of cantaloupe soup and the fruit mixture until well-chilled, at least 2 hours.

3. To serve, stir the club soda into the cantaloupe soup. Spoon the soup into individual soup bowls and sprinkle with the mint. Serve chilled, with the fruit mixture passed on the side.

Strawberry and Rum Tiramisù

Makes 6 to 8 servings

You won't believe how easy this is to make. There are many tiramisù recipes that are more complicated, but few that are better. Mascarpone, Italian ladyfingers, and instant espresso coffee powder can be found at Italian grocers and many supermarkets.

1 tablespoon instant espresso coffee powder
2 tablespoons granulated sugar
$\frac{1}{3}$ cup dark rum
One 17-ounce container mascarpone cheese (2 cups), at room temperature
$\frac{1}{2}$ cup confectioners' sugar
1 cup heavy cream
1 teaspoon vanilla extract
One 7-ounce package dry Italian ladyfingers (*savoiardi*)
1 pint fresh strawberries, stemmed and thinly sliced

1. Bring $\frac{3}{4}$ cup water to a boil in a small saucepan over high heat. Remove from the heat and stir in the espresso and granulated sugar to dissolve the sugar. Stir in $\frac{3}{4}$ cup cold water and the rum. Pour into a medium bowl and cool completely.

2. In another medium bowl, mash the mascarpone and confectioners' sugar with a rubber spatula, until combined. In a chilled bowl, whip the cream and vanilla just until soft peaks form. Fold the whipped cream into the mascarpone.

3. One at a time, briefly dip the ladyfingers into the espresso mixture (do not soak them—it takes only a second), and arrange in a single layer in an 11-inch by 8-inch dish, breaking the ladyfingers as needed to fit. Fill any gaps with pieces of ladyfingers, but don't get obsessive about it. Spread with half of the mascarpone mixture, then top with the sliced strawberries. Dip and layer the remaining ladyfingers, and spread with the remaining mascarpone. Discard the leftover espresso mixture.

4. Cover the tiramisù and refrigerate for at least 4 hours or overnight. To serve, spoon into bowls or large wineglasses.

Old-Fashioned Strawberry Shortcakes

Makes 8 servings

Strawberry shortcake has to hold the blue ribbon as everyone's favorite summer dessert. Here's a homemade version that blows mixes out of the water. Using two kinds of flour makes the shortcakes really tender.

BERRIES

2 pints fresh strawberries, stemmed and sliced
$\frac{1}{3}$ cup sugar

SHORTCAKE

1 cup cake flour (not self-rising)
1 cup all-purpose flour
2 tablespoons plus 1 teaspoon sugar
1 tablespoon baking powder
$\frac{1}{4}$ teaspoon salt
8 tablespoons (1 stick) unsalted butter, chilled and cut into $\frac{1}{4}$-inch cubes
$\frac{3}{4}$ cup half-and-half, plus more for brushing

TOPPING

2 cups heavy cream
$\frac{1}{4}$ cup sugar
1 teaspoon vanilla extract

1. To make the berry filling, combine the strawberries and sugar in a medium bowl. Cover and refrigerate until the berries release their juices, at least 3 hours, or overnight.

2. To make the shortcake, position a rack in the center of the oven and preheat to 400° F. Sift the flours, 2 tablespoons of the sugar, baking powder, and salt into a medium bowl. Using a pastry blender or 2 knives, cut the butter into the flour mixture until it resembles coarse meal. (You may pulse the mixture in a food processor, but transfer it to a medium bowl. Do not make the dough in the food processor bowl, or it will be tough.) Tossing the mixture with a fork, add the $^3/_4$ cup half-and-half, mixing until it forms a soft dough. Knead the dough in the bowl a few times until it is smooth. Do not overhandle the dough.

3. Press the dough into an ungreased 9-inch pie plate. Using a knife, mark the top of the dough into 8 wedges, making the marks about $^1/_4$ inch deep. Brush the top with a little half-and-half and sprinkle lightly with the remaining 1 teaspoon sugar. Bake until the shortcake is golden brown, and a toothpick inserted in the center comes out clean, about 25 minutes. Cool for 5 minutes in the pan, then invert onto a wire cake rack, turn right side up, and cool completely.

4. To serve, whip the cream, sugar, and vanilla in a chilled, large bowl until stiff peaks form. Using a serrated knife, split the shortcake. Cut through the markings on the top half to make 8 shortcake wedges. Set the top aside. Place the bottom half—still in one piece—on a serving plate. Heap about two-thirds of the berries, with their juices, onto the shortcake bottom. Spread half of the whipped cream over the berries. Place the 8 shortcake wedges, in their original order, on top. Cut through the bottom shortcake to make 8 individual servings. Serve immediately with the remaining berries and whipped cream passed on the side.

Blueberry Coffee Cake

Makes 6 to 8 servings

Although my main interest is healthy eating, desserts like this one are okay if balanced with low-fat ones. We all need some comfort foods once in a while. After a busy night in the firehouse, a hot cup of coffee and a small piece of this cake make you feel good. Many years ago, the original version of this recipe was published in Marian Burros's *New York Times* food column, and ever since, New Yorkers have been passing the recipe back and forth. Some people make it with plums, peaches, or apples, but I like it with blueberries.

> 1 scant cup all-purpose flour (spoon the flour lightly into a measuring cup, then level with the side of a knife)
> 1 tablespoon baking powder
> $^1/_8$ teaspoon salt
> 8 tablespoons (1 stick) unsalted butter, softened
> $^3/_4$ cup plus 1 teaspoon sugar
> 2 large eggs
> 1 teaspoon vanilla extract
> 1 cup fresh blueberries
> $^1/_8$ teaspoon cinnamon

1. Position a rack in the center of the oven and preheat to 350° F. Lightly butter a 9-inch round cake pan.

2. In a small bowl, whisk to combine the flour, baking powder, and salt. Set aside.

3. Using an electric mixer at high speed, beat the butter and $^3/_4$ cup of the sugar until light and fluffy, about 2 minutes. One at a time, beat in the eggs, then the vanilla. On low speed, beat in the flour mixture just until combined. Do not overmix.

4. Spread the batter evenly in the prepared pan. Scatter the blueberries on top. Sprinkle with the remaining 1 teaspoon sugar and the cinnamon.

5. Bake for 40 to 45 minutes, until the top is golden brown and a toothpick inserted in the center comes out clean. Cool in the pan on a wire cake rack.

Mango and Raspberry Cobbler

Makes 8 servings

Ripe, juicy mangoes make a fantastic cobbler. Look for ripe mangoes that yield slightly when squeezed. If you wish, serve this with scoops of ice cream.

FILLING

6 ripe large mangoes, pitted, peeled and cut into $\frac{1}{2}$-inch-thick slices
    (see Note)
$1\frac{1}{2}$ cups sugar
2 tablespoons cornstarch
2 tablespoons fresh lime juice
Three 6-ounce baskets fresh raspberries
6 tablespoons ($\frac{3}{4}$ stick) unsalted butter, cut into pieces

TOPPING

$1\frac{3}{4}$ cups all-purpose flour
$\frac{1}{3}$ cup sugar
1 tablespoon baking powder
$\frac{1}{2}$ teaspoon salt
8 tablespoons (1 stick) unsalted butter, chilled and cut into pieces
1 large egg
Approximately $\frac{1}{2}$ cup milk

1. Position a rack in the center of the oven and preheat to 400° F.

2. To make the filling, toss the mango slices, sugar, cornstarch, and lime juice in a large bowl. Gently stir in the raspberries. Transfer to a 9-inch by 13-inch baking dish and dot with the butter.

3. To make the topping: Sift the flour, sugar, baking powder, and salt into a large bowl. Using a pastry blender, cut in the butter until it looks like small peas. In a small glass measuring cup, combine the egg and enough milk to measure $\frac{3}{4}$ cup. Beat until well combined. Stir into the dry ingredients to make a soft dough—do not overmix. Drop large spoonfuls of the dough randomly over the top of the fruit.

4. Bake, covering the top with foil if it seems to be browning too quickly, until a toothpick inserted in the topping comes out clean and the juices are bubbling, about 45 minutes. Serve warm.

Note: To peel a mango, lay a ripe mango on a work surface, plump side down. The mango pit is long and flat, and runs horizontally through the fruit. Using a sharp, thin-bladed knife, slice off the top third of the mango, cutting over and around the pit. Turn the mango over and slice off the other side. One piece at a time, using a large serving spoon, scoop out the mango flesh in one piece from the peel. Cut the peeled mango lengthwise into $\frac{1}{2}$-inch slices.

Lemon Mist Pie

Makes 8 servings

I'm not a baker, so I depend on crumb crusts to get me through the pie-making process. This is my "make-with-your-eyes-closed" version of lemon cream pie.

CRUST

1 cup (about 5 ounces) graham cracker crumbs
$\frac{1}{4}$ cup sugar
4 tablespoons ($\frac{1}{2}$ stick) unsalted butter, melted

FILLING

One 14-ounce can sweetened condensed milk
5 large egg yolks
$\frac{1}{2}$ cup fresh lemon juice
Grated zest of 1 lemon

TOPPING

$\frac{1}{2}$ cup heavy cream
1 tablespoon sugar

1. Position a rack in the center of the oven and preheat to 350° F.

2. To make the crust, combine the cracker crumbs and sugar in a medium bowl. Stir in the melted butter until the crumbs are moistened. Press firmly and evenly into a 9-inch pie pan. Bake until the crust looks set, about 5 minutes. Do not overbake. Remove the crust from the oven.

3. To make the filling, in a medium bowl, use an electric mixer at high speed and beat the condensed milk, egg yolks, lemon juice, and lemon zest until well combined. Pour into the crust. Bake until the filling looks set about 25 minutes. Place the pie on a wire cake rack and cool completely. Cover and refrigerate until well chilled, at least 2 hours or overnight.

4. To make the topping, in a chilled, medium bowl, whip the cream and sugar until soft peaks form. Spread over the chilled pie. Serve immediately, or cover with plastic wrap and keep refrigerated until ready to serve.

Peanut Butter and Chocolate Cookie Pie

PEGGY THOMAS AND FIREFIGHTER CHUCK WILLARD ▪ **JOLIET FIRE DEPARTMENT** ▪ **JOLIET, ILLINOIS**

Makes 8 servings

Peggy writes *The City Slicker*, a newsletter for the Joliet Police and Fire-fighters. Every month, she features recipes from my first book, and I'm happy to return the favor and print one of hers, submitted by Firefighter Chuck Willard. Low-fat, it isn't. But, it tastes great, so keep the portions small.

CRUST

1 cup (5 ounces) chocolate wafer cookie crumbs (crush in a food
    processor or blender)
$\frac{1}{4}$ cup sugar
4 tablespoons ($\frac{1}{2}$ stick) unsalted butter, melted

8 ounces cream cheese, softened
1 cup sugar
1 cup smooth peanut butter
1 tablespoon unsalted butter, at room temperature
1 cup heavy cream
$\frac{1}{3}$ cup mini-chocolate chips

1. Position a rack in the center of the oven and preheat to 350° F.

2. To make the crust, combine the cookie crumbs and sugar in a medium bowl. Stir in the melted butter until the crumbs are moistened. Press firmly and evenly into a 9-inch pie pan. Bake until the crust looks dry and set, about 10 minutes. Cool completely.

3. To make the filling, in a medium bowl, use an electric mixer to beat the cream cheese and sugar until well-combined, about 1 minute. Add the peanut butter and butter and mix well.

4. In a chilled, medium bowl, whip the cream until soft peaks begin to form. Fold into the peanut butter mixture. Spread into the cooled crust and sprinkle with the mini-chips.

5. Cover with plastic wrap and chill until firm, at least 4 hours or overnight. Serve chilled.

Double-Decker Cheesecake Brownies

Makes 12 brownies

Brownies are always a hit with firefighters, unless you're serving cheesecake. So, why not mix up both and guarantee success?

BROWNIE

$1/2$ cup all-purpose flour
$1/4$ teaspoon baking soda
$1/4$ teaspoon salt
6 tablespoons ($3/4$ stick) unsalted butter, cut into pieces
3 ounces unsweetened chocolate, finely chopped
1 cup sugar
2 large eggs
1 teaspoon vanilla extract

CHEESECAKE LAYER

One 8-ounce package cream cheese, softened
2 tablespoons unsalted butter, softened
2 tablespoons sugar
1 large egg
2 tablespoons all-purpose flour
$1/2$ teaspoon vanilla extract

1. Position a rack in the center of the oven and preheat to 350° F. Line an 8-inch square baking pan with aluminum foil so the foil extends 2 inches over the two opposite ends of the pan. Fold the overhang down to form "handles." Butter the bottom of the foil-lined pan.

2. To make the brownie, whisk to combine the flour, baking soda, and salt in a medium bowl and set aside.

3. In a medium saucepan, melt the butter over medium heat. Remove from the heat and add the chocolate. Let stand until softened, about 3 minutes, then whisk until smooth. Let stand until tepid, about 10 minutes. Whisk in the sugar.

One at a time, whisk in the eggs, then the vanilla. Using a wooden spoon, stir in the flour mixture. Spread evenly in the prepared pan. Place in the freezer while preparing cheesecake mixture.

4. To make the cheesecake layer, in a medium bowl, use an electric mixer set at medium speed to beat the cream cheese, butter, and sugar until smooth, about 1 minute. Beat in the egg, flour, and vanilla.

5. Spread the cheesecake layer evenly over the brownie layer. Bake until the edges of the cheesecake layer have risen and set, 30 to 35 minutes. (The center may look wet, but will firm upon standing.) Cool completely on a wire cake rack. Lift up on the foil handles to remove the brownie from the pan. Cut the brownie into squares.

Chocolate Chocolate Chip Biscotti

Makes about 36 biscotti

These double-chocolate biscotti can be nibbled on their own, dunked into iced coffee, or served with a bowl of summer berries.

1 ounce unsweetened chocolate, finely chopped
8 tablespoons (1 stick) unsalted butter, at room temperature
1 cup sugar
2 large eggs
1 teaspoon vanilla extract
2 cups plus 2 tablespoon all-purpose flour
1 teaspoon baking powder
$\frac{1}{4}$ teaspoon salt
$\frac{1}{2}$ cup mini-chocolate chips

1. Position the racks in the top and center of the oven and preheat to 350° F.

2. Place the chocolate in a heatproof bowl and place over a saucepan of very hot, but not simmering, water. Let stand until the chocolate is melted, about 3 minutes. (Or, microwave at Medium power—50 percent—until it looks shiny, about $1\frac{1}{2}$ minutes. Let stand for 1 minute, then stir until melted.) Remove from the heat and let cool to tepid, but still liquid.

3. In a medium bowl, using an electric mixer at high speed, beat the butter and sugar until light and fluffy, about 2 minutes. One at a time, beat in the eggs. Beat in the cooled chocolate and the vanilla.

4. In another medium bowl, whisk to combine the flour, baking powder, and salt. On low speed, gradually beat the flour mixture into the chocolate mixture to make a smooth dough. Stir in the mini-chips.

5. Using lightly floured hands on a lightly floured work surface, form the dough into two 10-inch by 2-inch rectangular logs. Place the logs at least 2 inches apart on an ungreased, large baking sheet. Bake in the center of the oven until the logs are set (press gently to check) and lightly browned, about 30 minutes. Remove from the oven and cool for 15 minutes.

6. Using a serrated knife, with a sawing motion carefully cut the logs into ½-inch diagonal slices, discarding the end pieces. Arrange the slices, cut sides down and close together on two baking sheets. Bake until the edges are lightly browned, 8 to 9 minutes. Turn the biscotti over, and switch the position of the baking sheets from top to bottom. Continue baking until the other sides are lightly browned, about 9 minutes longer. Cool completely.

Strawberry Lemonade

Makes 3 quarts (about 12 servings)

Parched? What quenches thirst better than lemonade? (Especially if it has strawberries in it, too.)

> 2 cups fresh lemon juice
> 1½ cups sugar
> 1 pint fresh strawberries, hulled

In a blender, process 1 cup of the lemon juice, the sugar, and strawberries until the strawberries are pureed and the sugar dissolves. Pour into a large pitcher. Add the remaining 1 cup lemon juice and 2 quarts ice water. Serve chilled.

Spiced and Iced Orange Tea

Makes 2 quarts (about 6 servings)

If you want crystal-clear iced tea, steep it in cold water. Tea made from boiled water will become cloudy when refrigerated.

> 2 oranges
> 6 tea bags orange pekoe tea
> $\frac{1}{3}$ cup sugar
> 3 cinnamon sticks
> 12 whole cloves
> 12 whole allspice berries

1. Using a vegetable peeler, remove the colored orange zest (not the bitter white pith beneath it) from 1 orange. Squeeze the juice from both oranges.

2. In a large pitcher, stir the tea bags, 2 quarts cold water, sugar, the orange juice and zest, cinnamon, cloves, and allspice. Cover and let stand at room temperature until the tea is brewed, at least 4 hours.

3. Strain the tea and return to the pitcher. Serve over ice cubes.

Summertime White Wine Sangría

Makes 6 servings

Raspberries and orange-flavored liqueur really spiff up this sangría. No need to use an expensive wine, but pick one that you would drink by itself—you can't make bad wine into good sangría.

> 1 seedless orange
> One 750-ml bottle dry white wine
> One 6-ounce basket fresh raspberries
> ¼ cup orange-flavored liqueur, such as Grand Marnier
> 1 cup sparkling water or club soda

1. Using a vegetable peeler, remove the colored orange zest (not the bitter white pith beneath it) from the orange and set aside. Cut away the thick white pith and discard. Cut the orange into thin rounds.

2. In a pitcher, mix the wine, raspberries, liqueur, orange rounds, and zest. Cover and refrigerate until well-chilled, at least 2 hours.

3. Just before serving, stir in the sparkling water. Serve immediately.

Index